To Brenda

Raves 'n Craves

Enjoy
Mae Adams

Copyright © 1985 by Mae Adams

All rights reserved. No part of this book may be reproduced in any form by any means without permission in writing from the author, except by a reviewer, who may quote brief passages in a review.

Canadian Cataloguing in Publication Data

    Adams, Mae
        Raves 'n craves

        Includes index.
        ISBN 0-88925-603-9

        1. Cookery.   1. Title
    TX715.A33 1985   641.5   C85-091312-8

Typeset by the Vancouver Courier

Printed and bound in Canada by Friesen Printers, Cloverdale, B.C. V3S 4C8.

Distributed by Raincoast Books,
112 East 3rd Avenue, Vancouver, B.C. V5T 1C8

CONTENTS

- **5 INTRODUCTION**
- **6 ACKNOWLEDGEMENTS**
- **7 APPETIZERS**
  - Dips and Dunks
  - Hors d'Oeuvres
  - Pates and Spreads
- **29 SALADS**
  - Green Salads
  - Hot Salads
  - Marinated Salads
- **51 VEGETABLES**
  - Potatoes
  - Skewered
  - Stir-Fried
  - Pickles and Jam
- **67 SOUPS**
  - Broth, also Stock
  - Hot Soups
- **79 SIDE DISHES**
  - Barley
  - Pasta
  - Rice
- **91 MEALS-in-ONE**
  - Breakfast and Brunch
  - Casseroles and Stews
  - Ethnic Dishes
- **115 ENTREES**
  - Fish and Seafood
  - Meats
  - Poultry
- **149 BREADS**
  - Muffins and Scones
  - Pancakes
  - Quick Breads
  - Yeast Breads
- **167 COOKIES**
  - Bars and Squares
  - Sweets
- **179 DESSERTS**
  - Berries and Fruit
  - Cakes and Tortes
  - Pies and Pastry
  - Puddings and Cobblers
- **204 RECIPE INDEX**

Dedicated to my parents
who nurtured my tastebuds
and
to my husband, Bob
whose support and encouragement
made my "dreams" come true.

INTRODUCTION

This is not a basic, everyday cookbook. Rather, it is a compilation of outstanding favourites which my family and I have enjoyed over the years. The "rave" recipes represent the best of the current and contemporary, culled from my weekly cooking column in the Vancouver Courier. Others were acquired throughout my travels down to New Orleans, and more recently, California.

Good, down-home cooking remains my passion and my preference. Thus, the "craves". I couldn't resist including the traditional stand-bys that brought so much joy to my own childhood. Creamy as can be rice pudding; scrumpets that literally melt in your mouth; and cinnamon buns you wouldn't believe.

From far and near, friends parted with their coveted favourites to add an extra delicious "lift" to my repertoire. I have carefully chosen those recipes which will appeal to a casual life-style of eating. There's nothing overly exotic or pretentious. Nor is there anything requiring days-on-end of preparation time.

I am hoping that my book will spark your imagination and provide you with more than just a little inspiration to lead you on the road to good cooking. Enjoy!

Mae Adams
Vancouver, 1985

ACKNOWLEDGEMENTS

Special thanks to Elizabeth Grant who diligently typeset my manuscript and to production manager, Rosemary Jones, whose talent and expertise in the graphics department at the Vancouver Courier made Raves 'n Craves such a winner. To Leanne Baker, a round of applause for the beautiful illustrations. Acknowledgements also go to all those who shared their great love for food within the pages of this book. You made my day!

Cover design by Tom Moore
and
Illustrations by Leanne Baker

COOL AS A CUCUMBER DIP

Chill: 2 hrs.
Makes: 2 cups/500 mL

Especially good with carrot sticks and thin Norwegian whole grain flatbread

¾	cup dairy sour cream	175 mL
4	oz. soft cream cheese	125 g
1	Tbs. good mayonnaise	15 mL
1	tsp. cider or wine vinegar	5 mL
½	tsp. seasoning salt (or to taste)	2 mL
¾	cup diced English cucumber	175 mL
¼	cup minced green onion	50 mL
	Minced parsley for garnish	

In mixing bowl, combine sour cream, cream cheese, mayonnaise, vinegar, and seasoning salt. Stir in cucumber and green onion. Transfer to serving bowl. Sprinkle with parsley. Cover and chill for at least 2 hours.

LAYERED NACHO DIP

Serves: 8-10

SUPERB! And so easy to make. Surround with plain nachos or tortilla triangles for some fanciful dipping.

1	tin refried beans	398 mL
2	lrg. avocados, peeled, pitted	2
1	Tbs. fresh lemon juice	15 mL
½	tsp. salt (or to taste)	2 mL
¼	tsp. pepper	1 mL
1½	cups dairy sour cream	375 mL
1	pkg. taco seasoning	35 g
1	cup grated Monterey Jack	250 mL
1	cup grated cheddar	250 mL
	Topping:	
3	med. tomatoes, seeded, diced	3
1	med. bunch green onions, chopped	1
1	cup pitted black olives, sliced	250 mL

1. Spread refried beans over bottom of large platter.
2. Mash avocado with fork. Add lemon juice and seasonings to taste. Spread over beans.
3. Combine sour cream and taco seasoning in small bowl. Spread evenly over avocado layer.
4. Sprinkle cheeses over sour cream mixture.
5. Arrange tomatoes, green onions, and ripe olives in whatever pattern you wish over cheese. Cover with plastic wrap and keep refrigerated until serving time.

ANTIPASTO

Chill: 12 hrs.
Serves: 10-12

Antipasto refers to "eats before the meal". This tomato-based hors d'oeuvre makes a handsome introduction to an Italian inspired menu. It may be served as a first course or as an appetizer served on crackers.

2	med. green peppers, chopped	2
2	med. ribs celery, chopped	2
2	med. carrots, in small rounds	2
¼	cup good olive oil	50 mL
1	cup tomato chili sauce	250 mL
1	cup catchup	250 mL
1	tin sliced mushrooms, drained	284 mL
1	cup sweet pickles, chopped	250 mL
1	cup tiny pickled onions	250 mL
½	cup pitted ripe olives, sliced	125 mL
½	cup stuffed olives, sliced	125 mL
Extras:		
1	tin solid tuna, drained	198 g
½	cup apple cider vinegar	125 mL

1. In a large heavy saucepan, heat olive oil. Add green pepper, celery, and carrots. Gently saute for 10 minutes.
2. Add chili sauce, catchup, mushrooms, pickles, onions, and olives. Simmer another 10 minutes, stirring occasionally.
3. Add tuna, breaking into large chunks. Stir in vinegar. Simmer until heated through. Transfer to glass container and refrigerate. Will keep for 1 week.

NOTE: Cauliflower florets, cut-up green beans, and artichoke hearts may be used to replace any of the above vegetables.

GUACAMOLE (Avocado Dip)

Makes: 2 cups/ 500 mL

Tostados and tacos just wouldn't be the same without this avocado delight. Be sure to plan ahead so that you will have ripe, not rock-hard avocados on hand. Serve with vegetable dippers and tortilla chips.

2	lrg. ripened avocados	2
2	tsp. fresh lemon juice	10 mL
½	tsp. salt (or to taste)	2 mL
¼	tsp. garlic powder	1 mL
¼	tsp. tabasco sauce*	1 mL
1	med. tomato, seeded, chopped	1
½	sm. onion, chopped	½

1. Peel and pit avocados. Save back one pit.
2. Mash avocado pulp coarsely with fork while mixing in the lemon juice. Add seasonings to your own taste. Fold in chopped tomato and onion.
3. Transfer guacamole to small serving bowl. Bury reserved pit in centre to help mixture from browning. Cover tightly with plastic and serve as soon as possible.

* A small green chili, seeded and finely minced may be used in place of the tabasco sauce.

SALMON BELLIES

Serves: 4

I doubt that there is a soul around who hasn't heard of the "Three Greenhorns" near English Bay. Owner, Fred Dalton is the only "Greenhorn" left, but his bill of fare still reflects Westcoast inspirations such as this one. "Salmon Bellies" was a recipe developed back in 1969 when the restaurant first opened. It's as popular today as it was then.

8	lrg. thin slices smoked salmon	8
	Filling:	
2	cups fresh tiny shrimp	500 mL
1	cup heavy cream, whipped	250 mL
2	Tbs. horseradish	25 mL
	Salt and pepper to taste	
	Garnish:	
½	head iceberg lettuce	½
1	lemon, cut into wedges	1
	Parsley sprigs	

1. Make filling first by combining shrimps, whipped cream, and horseradish. Season lightly with salt and pepper.
2. Divide mixture into 8 portions and place on salmon slices. Roll into cornets (like cones).
3. Finely shave the lettuce (do this last minute to prevent browning) and place on 4 platters. Arrange 2 cornets per serving on top of lettuce with lemon wedges and parsley sprigs for garnish.

LIVER and MUSHROOM PATE

Chill: 8 hr.
Serves: 8

A favourite from my good friend, Mary Bell. This is a smooth liver pate requiring the use of a processor or blender.

2	Tbs. butter or margarine	25 mL
8	oz. fresh chicken livers	250 g
¼	lb. fresh mushrooms, sliced	125 g
¼	cup chopped green onions	50 mL
⅓	cup dry white wine	75 mL
1	med. clove garlic, minced	1
½	tsp. salt (or to taste)	2 mL
¼	tsp. dry mustard	1 mL
¼	tsp. dried rosemary leaves	1 mL
¼	tsp. dried dillweed	1 mL
¼	cup soft butter	50 mL

1. In a wide skillet, melt butter. Add cut-up livers, mushrooms, and onions, sauteing just until liver loses its pinkness.
2. Add wine, garlic, salt, mustard, and herbs. Cover and simmer gently for 10 minutes.
3. Uncover and cook until most of the liquid has dissipated. Cool slightly and place in processor or blender. Whirl until smooth.
4. Add soft butter and continue to whirl until mixture is satiny smooth. Taste for seasonings. Turn into crock. Chill at least 8 hours or overnight. Will keep refrigerated for 1 week.

PICKLED MUSHROOMS

Makes: 1 pt./ ½ L

Marvellous marinated. Prepare mushrooms by wiping with a damp cloth or quickly rinsing and patting dry. Never soak them as they are porous and will readily absorb the liquid surrounding them.

1	lb. medium-size mushrooms	500 g
	Boiling water — Juice of lemon	
1	sm. onion, thinly sliced	1
	Marinade:	
1	cup cider vinegar	250 mL
1	med. clove garlic, crushed	1
1	Tbs. granulated sugar	15 mL
1	tsp. salt	5 mL
1	med. bay leaf	1
½	tsp. dried thyme leaves	2 mL
½	tsp. cracked peppercorns	2 mL
½	cup vegetable oil	125 mL
1	Tbs. minced parsley	15 mL

1. Clean and trim mushrooms, leaving on stems. Place in a medium saucepan with hot water to cover. Add juice of lemon. Bring to a quick boil. Cook for 2 minutes.
2. Drain mushrooms in colander. Then layer with onion slices in a 1 pt./½ L glass container. Set aside.
3. In a small saucepan, combine vinegar, garlic, sugar, salt, bay leaf, thyme, and peppercorns. Bring to a boil. Reduce heat and let simmer gently for about 5 minutes.
4. Remove mixture from heat and stir in oil and parsley. Pour it over mushrooms and onions while still hot. Cool completely. Cover and then chill overnight.
5. Before serving, drain and sprinkle mushrooms and onions with a little extra parsley. Serve with picks.

PISMO BEACH CLAM TIDBITS

Serves: 4-6

An adaptation of a recipe I acquired from Trader Vic's during their "California Native Foods" celebration. You'll love the cool crunch of lettuce contrasted with the hot spiciness of sauteed chiles, pork, chopped vegetables, and clams.

	Lettuce leaves or endive petals	
	Filling:	
2	Tbs. cooking oil	25 mL
1	sm. chili pepper, seeded, minced	1
6	oz. coarsely ground raw pork	200 g
½	lb. fresh mushrooms, chopped	250 g
¼	cup chopped bamboo shoots	50 mL
¼	cup chopped peeled waterchestnuts	50 mL
¼	cup juice drained from clams	50 mL
½	cup tinned baby clams, drained	125 mL
2	Tbs. oyster-flavoured sauce	25 mL
	Salt and pepper to taste	
2	green onions, finely chopped	2

1. Separate lettuce leaves. Rinse and pat dry. Keep chilled until serving time.
2. In a wide, heavy skillet (cast iron is excellent), heat oil until hot. Add chopped chili and stir 1-2 minutes. Then add pork, mixing over high heat until browned.
3. Add chopped vegetables and the clam juice, stirring until most of the liquid has been reduced (almost dry).
4. Stir in the clams and oyster sauce with salt and pepper to taste. Mixture should be heated through and remain moist and crunchy. Keep hot.
5. Just before serving, add green onions. Place mixture in serving bowl with lettuce leaves surrounding it. Let each guest help himself.

PUB-STYLE PICKLED EGGS

Yields: 12 lrg.

12	lrg. eggs, hard-cooked	12
1	med. onion, in rings	1
	Marinade:	
1½	cups regular white vinegar	375 mL
½	cup water	125 mL
2	Tbs. granulated sugar	25 mL
2	tsp. whole pickling spice	10 mL
1	tsp. salt	5 mL

1. Shell eggs and place in large glass jar along with the onion rings.
2. In a medium stainless saucepan, combine all the marinade items. Bring to a boil; then reduce heat and let mixture simmer 5 minutes.
3. Immediately pour over eggs and onions. Cover and refrigerate for 24 hours. Eggs will keep under refrigeration for up to 2 weeks.

NOTE: For easier shelling, stash away a carton of eggs in the back of the fridge for a good week or two before cooking. Somehow, fresh-from-the-farm eggs do not peel well.

For a simple, rustic meal, accompany these eggs with freshly-baked bread, a chunk of good cheddar, and a tankard of foaming beer or ale. Pickled eggs are also delicious served with salads and cold cuts.

RED ONION-PARSLEY ROUNDS

Makes about 40

Simple, but always a smash hit with the cocktail crowd. Though red onion does add a festive touch, any mild variety such as Spanish or Maui will do. Have your favourite bakery slice a white sandwich loaf thinly into lengthwise slabs.

1	loaf bread, sliced lengthwise	1
½	cup soft butter or margarine	125 mL
1	med. red onion, finely chopped	1
1	cup good mayonnaise	250 mL
2	cups finely minced parsley	500 mL
	Watercress leaves for garnish	

1. Using cookie cutter, cut bread into small rounds, about 2 in./5 cm in diameter. Spread half with soft butter and then sprinkle with red onion bits. Top with unbuttered rounds to form sandwiches.

2. Roll edges of each in mayonnaise and then in minced parsley. Arrange on large tray in single layer. Cover and chill for at least 1 hour. Serve, surrounded by watercress sprigs for nibbling.

RED SALMON PATE

Chill: 4 hrs.
Makes: 1 cup/250 mL

1	sm. tin red salmon, drained	106 g
4	oz. soft cream cheese	125 g
2	Tbs. butter or margarine	25 mL
1	Tbs. minced green onion	15 mL
1	tsp. fresh lemon juice	5 mL
	Salt and pepper to taste	

1. Remove skin and bones from salmon, if you wish. Mash salmon well with fork. Mix in remaining ingredients with seasonings to taste. Pate should be very smooth.
2. Pack mixture into a crock. Chill several hours before serving. Will keep refrigerated for several days.

Serve this tasty pate on cucumber rounds, party bread, or crisp crackers. Then top with chopped smoked salmon or lox and a light sprinkling of minced parsley. May also be used to stuff cherry tomatoes.

CHERRY TOMATO APPETIZERS: Use large, firm cherry tomatoes. Place stem-side down and cut each into sixth's (not quite through to bottom), so that each resembles a flower with petals. Scoop out seeds and water and centre each with a whole pitted black olive or well-drained smoked oyster. Sprinkle with a nip of minced parsley. Tasty and impressive.

ROASTED PEPPER-CREAM CHEESE DIP

Makes: 1 cup/250 mL

Serve with vegetable dippers and crisp breads.

1	sm. green pepper, roasted*	1
4	oz. soft cream cheese	125 g
½	cup dairy sour cream	125 mL
½	sm. mild onion, minced	½
½	tsp. Worcestershire sauce	2 mL
¼	tsp. cayenne pepper	1 mL
¼	tsp. salt (or to taste)	1 mL
	Minced chives or parsley	

1. Roast pepper as directed below. Chop finely and set aside.
2. In mixing bowl, beat cream cheese, sour cream, onion, Worcestershire, cayenne, and salt until smooth and well blended.
3. Stir in roasted pepper bits. Transfer to serving container. Garnish with minced chives or parsley. Cover and chill until serving time.

* To roast bell pepper: Wash pepper. Leave whole and char over open flame or under broiler (about 4 in./10 cm from heat source). Roast, turning with tongs until skin is blistered and tinged with brown. This will take about 15 minutes. Enclose pepper in paper bag to "sweat" for 15-20 minutes. Run under cold water, slipping off skin. Remove stem-end and seeds.

SASSY EGGPLANT DIP (Processor)

Chill: 4-6 hrs.
Yields: 2 cups/500 mL

Thanks to Sheila Anzurut for introducing me to this one. Delicious served with an array of fresh veggies.

2	lrg. eggplants, unpeeled	2
1	cup packed parsley sprigs	250 mL
½	sm. onion, chopped	½
1	med. clove garlic, minced	1
½	cup mayonnaise (homemade)	125 mL
2	tsp. fresh lemon juice	10 mL
1	tsp. salt (or to taste)	5 mL
½	tsp. dried basil leaves	2 mL
½	tsp. dried oregano leaves	2 mL
½	tsp. dried dillweed	2 mL
½	tsp. Dijon-style mustard	2 mL
¼	tsp. pepper	1 mL

1. Pierce eggplants a couple of times with paring knife. Place in shallow pan and bake in preheated 350F/180C oven for 1 hour. Turn occasionally until softened. Cool. Peel off skin. Cut into chunks. Set aside.

2. Mince parsley in processor using steel knife. With machine running, add onion and garlic until well minced. Add eggplant chunks and puree, scraping down sides of bowl.

3. Add remaining ingredients, letting machine run for 5 seconds or until mixture is smooth and well blended.

4. Spoon into an attractive serving dish. Cover. Chill until serving time. Excellent with thinly sliced jicama, cucumbers, and carrots. Also try parboiled brussels sprouts and green beans.

MAYONNAISE for DIP

Makes: 1 cup/250mL

1	lrg. whole egg	1
1	lrg. egg yolk (opt.)	1
2	tsp. fresh lemon juice	10 mL
1	tsp. red wine vinegar	5 mL
1	tsp. Dijon mustard	5 mL
½	tsp. salt (or to taste)	2 mL
¼	tsp. pepper	1 mL
¼	cup good olive oil	50 mL
¾	cup safflo or salad oil	175 mL

1. In a food processor, combine whole egg and yolk (both at room temperature), lemon juice, vinegar, mustard, salt and pepper, and olive oil. Turn machine on and off to blend until slightly thickened.
2. With machine running, add safflo in a slow, steady stream through feed tube JUST until thickened. Do not over-process, otherwise mayonnaise will separate. Store in glass jar and keep refrigerated.

NOTE: If emulsion separates, it can be rescued by starting anew with an egg yolk, lemon juice, vinegar, and mustard; and then gradually adding separated mayonnaise to the egg-acid mixture in place of additional oil.

Two secrets to making a well-emulsified mayonnaise: (1) Have all the ingredients at room temperature, and (2) Add the oil to the egg-acid base in a thin, constant stream just until thickened. Over-beating or over-processing will cause the mixture to separate. Homemade mayonnaise makes a superb base for all kinds of dips and dressings eg. Green Herbed Mayonnaise, Curry Mayonnaise, Thousand Island Dressing, and Green Goddess Dressing.

GRAVAD LAX (Marinated Salmon)

Marinate: 48 hrs.
Serves: 6-8

2	lb. centre-cut red salmon	1 kg
3	Tbs. coarse salt	50 mL
¼	cup granulated sugar	50 mL
1	Tbs. crushed peppercorns	15 mL
1	lrg. bunch fresh dill, sprigs	1

This is a Swedish delicacy somewhat resembling the Kosher-style lox. Here, the salmon must be absolutely fresh (not frozen) and must also be filleted — that is, deboned. The flesh is then sprinkled with fresh dill sprigs, coarse salt (either Kosher or sea salt), sugar, and crushed peppercorns; and left to marinate in the refrigerator for 48 hours or up to 3 days. Traditionally, gravad lax is served thinly sliced, as an appetizer or as part of a smorgasbord. It is usually accompanied with a mustard sauce, such as the one below and buttered dark bread.

1. Separate salmon into 2 flat pieces. Debone, leaving on skin. Pat dry.
2. Combine salt, sugar, and peppercorns. Sprinkle over flesh. Scatter dill on top, leaving some for outside. Slap salmon halves together, flesh-side together.
3. Lay salmon on bed of reserved dill on heavy foil. Cover with a little more dill. Wrap tightly and set on rimmed platter. Weigh down with brick or other heavy object.
4. Refrigerate for 2-3 days, turning occasionally. When ready, scrape off dill and seasonings. Slice very thin on the bias, detaching each slice from skin. Serve with mustard sauce. Gravad lax will keep for 1 week, chilled.

MUSTARD DILL SAUCE: In a small bowl, combine 3 Tbs./50 mL prepared brown mustard, 1 Tbs./15 mL EACH of granulated sugar and white vinegar, and 1 tsp./5 mL dry mustard. Add ¼ cup/50 mL salad oil in a thin stream, whisking constantly until thick and smooth. Stir in 2 Tbs./25 mL chopped fresh dillweed. Cover and refrigerate several hours. Makes about ½ cup/125 mL.

LEMON TOMATO SAUSAGE BITES

Serves: 6

Also delicious with cocktail-size meatballs.

1	lb. pkg. skinless pork sausages	500 g
	Vegetable oil for cooking	
	Sauce:	
1	sm. tin tomato sauce	213 mL
3	Tbs. brown sugar	50 mL
½	tsp. grated lemon rind	2 mL
2	Tbs. fresh lemon juice	25 mL
1	Tbs. white vinegar	15 mL
½	tsp. Worcestershire sauce	2 mL
¼	tsp. salt (or to taste)	1 mL

1. Brown sausages in a little oil. Drain well. Cut into bite-size pieces. Set aside.
2. Combine all sauce ingredients in medium saucepan. Let simmer for about 10 minutes. May be made ahead, but reheat.
3. Add sausages and heat through. Serve hot with toothpicks for spearing.

ZIPPY CLAM DUNK

Serves: 6

A tasty hot dunk to welcome your guests as they come from out of the cold.

1	med. green pepper, finely chopped	1
1	sm. onion, finely chopped	1
3	Tbs. butter or margarine	50 mL
1	tin baby clams, drained	142 g
¼	cup processed cheese, diced	50 mL
¼	cup catchup	50 mL
1	Tbs. Worcestershire sauce	15 mL
1	Tbs. dry sherry (maybe more)	15 mL
¼	tsp. cayenne	1 mL

1. In top part of double boiler, melt butter over direct heat and saute green pepper and onion, 8-10 minutes.
2. Remove from heat and add the remaining ingredients with cayenne (to taste).
3. Place pot over simmering water and cook until mixture is well blended. At this point, may be made ahead and reheated.
4. Transfer to chafing dish and keep hot. Add more sherry if mixture seems a little thick. Serve with crisp crackers.

SALSA MEXICANA

Makes: 2 cups/500 mL

1	lb. tomatoes (4 small)	500 g
1	sm. onion, chopped	1
1	med. clove garlic, minced	1
2	sm. chili peppers, chopped	2
3	Tbs. chopped fresh coriander*	50 mL
½	tsp. salt (or to taste)	2 mL

Chop tomatoes finely and combine with remaining ingredients. Let stand 1 hour for flavours to blend.

* If fresh coriander or cilantro is unavailable, you may use fresh parsley, however the flavour will not be the same.

"Salsa" is the Spanish word for sauce. It is a standard feature on most Mexican menus and may appear in the cooked or uncooked state. We prefer the latter. Hotness will depend on the type and amount of chili peppers. If you wish a mild salsa, use fewer chilies and remove the seeds (use caution so that the volatile oils do not get into your eyes). Good as a dip for nachos or as a condiment spooned over potato skins, tacos, or egg dishes.

TERRINE of PORK and VEAL with PISTACHIOS

Oven: 350F/180C
Bake: 1½ hrs.
Serves: 10-12

A terrine is just one of several names given to a glorified meat loaf (pate) baked in a deep, lidded mold, usually earthenware. French chefs like to use thin strips of salty pork fat for lining the terrine so as to give the pate a classic look and to also add extra flavour. Bacon (not too heavily smoked) serves our purpose well. If you do not have a terrine mold, a loaf pan makes a fine substitute.

8	thin slices bacon	8
1	med. chicken breast half	1
2	Tbs. cognac or dry sherry	25 mL
2	Tbs. butter or margarine	25 mL
1	med. onion, minced	1
1	med. clove garlic, minced	1
1	med. shallot, finely minced	1
1	lb. ground fresh pork	500 g
1	lb. ground fresh veal	500 g
2	lrg. eggs, beaten	2
1½	tsp. salt	7 mL
½	tsp. cracked peppercorns	2 mL
½	tsp. thyme leaves	2 mL
¼	tsp. nutmeg	1 mL
¼	tsp. allspice	1 mL
¼	cup shelled pistachio nuts	50 mL
3	med. bay leaves, whole	3
	More crushed peppercorns	

1. Line a terrine or 9x5 in./2 L loaf pan with bacon strips running crosswise and overlapping sides of pan.

2. Skin and bone chicken breast. Cut meat into 6 long strips. Sprinkle with cognac and let stand 30 minutes.

3. In small skillet, melt the butter and add minced onion, garlic, and shallot. Saute gently until tender, about 8 minutes.

4. Place sauteed mixture in mixing bowl with ground meat, eggs, seasonings, and herbs. Mix well.

5. Place half of the pate mixture in pan. Lay marinated chicken strips in long rows on top and then sprinkle pistachios over.

6. Cover with remaining meat. Fold bacon ends over top to encase filling. Arrange bay leaves on top. Generously sprinkle top of pate with more crushed peppercorns. Cover with foil.

7. Preheat oven. Place loaf in larger pan of hot water. Bake about 1½ hours or until pate shrinks away from sides of pan and juices no longer run pink.

8. Remove foil. Cool completely. Then pour off liquid and refrigerate to chill completely. Pate is best after a day or two. Serve in thin slices with party rye or croustines.

CUMBERLAND SAUCE

Yields: 1 cup/250 mL

Good served with ham or the above terrine.

1	med. orange, rind & juice	1
1	cup Port or Madeira	250 mL
1	Tbs. fresh lemon juice	15 mL
½	cup currant jelly	125 mL
	Pinch cayenne or ground ginger	

Finely shred orange rind and place in saucepan with wine. Cook over medium heat until mixture is reduced to ⅓ cup/75 mL. Add orange and lemon juices, jelly, and cayenne. Stir until jelly is melted. Serve hot or cold.

JALAPENO PEPPER JELLY

Yields: 6 jars

1	cup seeded, cut-up bell peppers	250 mL
½	cup seeded, cut-up chile peppers	125 mL
½	cup Japanese rice vinegar*	125 mL
1	cup cider vinegar	250 mL
6	cups granulated sugar	1.5 L
6	oz. bottle fruit pectin	750 mL

Red or green food colouring
Sterilized jars — Melted paraffin

1. Combine both peppers and rice vinegar in blender or processor. Cover and whirl for 30 seconds until finely minced.

2. Transfer to large (important) stainless pot. Stir in cider vinegar and the sugar (no skimping!). Cook and stir over medium heat until mixture comes to a boil. Skim off froth (important).

3. When mixture becomes impossible to stir down, add the pectin and let boil hard for 1 minute. Remove from heat and if desired, add 5-6 drops of colouring depending on the colour of the bell peppers.

4. Immediately ladle into prepared jars — not quite to the top. Use a clean knife to mix pulp throughout. Cover with melted paraffin. The recipe may be halved, but not doubled.

* If you cannot find Japanese rice vinegar, use cider vinegar. Rice vinegar has a mild, pleasing flavour which also makes it excellent for salads.

It takes almost no time to make this terrific-tasting jelly with a blender or processor. Dabbed over crispbreads and cream cheese, it makes a pretty special hors d'oeuvres for festive entertaining. Also super-good served as a condiment with roast pork or anything barbecued. Jalapeno chiles add to the fieriness of the jelly, and extreme caution is advised when using them. Wear rubber gloves to remove the seeds and do not let the volatile oils come into contact with eyes. Cold water is the only relief that I know.

SPIRITED ITALIAN SALAD

Chill: 2 hrs.
Serves: 6-8

Now here's a hearty main course salad that's ideal for the outdoors. It must be made ahead to let the flavours mingle.

1	tin garbanzo beans	398 mL
½	cup sliced pitted olives	125 mL
1	sm. green pepper, diced	1
1	sm. rib celery, chopped	1
Dressing:		
½	cup olive oil	125 mL
½	cup wine vinegar	125 mL
1	lrg. clove garlic, minced	1
1	tsp. dried leaf basil	5 mL
1	tsp. salt (or to taste)	5 mL
½	tsp. freshly ground pepper	2 mL
Garnishings:		
4	oz. salami, in strips	125 g
2	tomatoes, seeded, diced	2
1	sm. sweet onion, chopped	1
2	Tbs. minced parsley	25 mL

1. Drain and rinse garbanzo beans. Pat dry. Combine in glass bowl with olives, green pepper, and celery.
2. Whisk together dressing ingredients until thick and well-blended. Pour over salad mixture, tossing to mix.
3. Top salad with salami strips, tomatoes, onion, and parsley. Cover and chill for at least 2 hours before serving.

JICAMA MEDLEY

Chill: 1 hr.
Serves: 4-6

Jicama, pronounced "hee-cah-mah", is a native of Mexico. It's a peculiar-looking light brown root vegetable resembling rutabaga. Peel it and you'll discover a firm, crisp, juicy inside that is almost apple-like.

2	cups peeled, diced jicama	500 mL
1	cup diced cucumber	250 mL
1	lrg. green pepper, diced	1
1	sm. mild onion, diced	1
	Dressing:	
¼	cup salad oil	50 mL
2	Tbs. red wine vinegar	25 mL
1	Tbs. minced parsley	15 mL
½	tsp. salt (or to taste)	2 mL
¼	tsp. pepper	1 mL

1. In a small glass serving bowl, combine diced jicama, cucumber, green pepper, and onion.
2. Combine the dressing ingredients in a screw-lid jar and shake well to blend. Pour over diced vegetables and toss lightly.
3. Chill salad for 1 hour. Drain off excess liquid. Nice served in lettuce cups.

CARROT-PINEAPPLE MOLD

Chill: 6 hrs
Serves: 8

Add this jelled salad to your Thanksgiving or Christmas Day spread. Given to me by Edie, my Mother-in-law who loved to cook.

1	sm. pkg. lemon gelatin	85 g
1¼	cups boiling water	300 mL
½	cup granulated sugar	125 mL
1	lrg. lemon, rind & juice	1
¼	tsp. salt	1 mL
1	tin crushed pineapple, drained	398 mL
2	med. carrots, finely shredded	2
1	cup heavy cream, whipped	250 mL

1. Place gelatin in mixing bowl. Add boiling water, stirring to completely dissolve the crystals. Stir in sugar, lemon rind and juice, and the salt. Mix well. Chill until consistency of unbeaten egg white, about 1 hour.

2. When the mixture has turned gelatinous but not yet set, add the well-drained pineapple and shredded carrots. Fold in whipped cream. Pour into lightly-oiled 4 cup/1 L mold or a regular glass bowl. Chill until firm. Unmold just before serving.

CATALINA CARROTS

Marinate: 24 hrs.
Serves: 6-8

You'll love the tangy sweetness of these carrots. Perfect for barbecues and buffet entertaining as they can be made in advance. And not only that; they're certain to add a dash of colour to the table.

2	lbs. carrots, sliced	1 kg
	Boiling water	
1	med. onion, in rings	1
1	med. green pepper, diced	1
	Dressing:	
1	sm. tin tomato sauce	213 mL
½	cup granulated sugar	125 mL
⅓	cup regular vinegar	75 mL
¼	cup salad oil	50 mL
1	tsp. Worcestershire sauce	5 mL
½	tsp. dry mustard	2 mL
½	tsp. salt (or to taste)	2 mL
¼	tsp. pepper	1 mL
	Garnish:	
2	Tbs. minced parsley	25 mL

1. Cook carrots in boiling water just until tender, but not falling apart. Drain well in colander. Place in large mixing bowl with onion rings and diced green pepper.
2. Whisk or blend together sauce ingredients until well blended. Pour over carrot mixture. Cover and let marinate in refrigerator for at least 24 hours.
3. Before serving, sprinkle with a little minced parsley.

DILLED CUCUMBERS

Marinate: 30 min.
Serves: 6-8

2	med. English cucumbers	2
2	tsp. salt	10 mL
½	cup white vinegar	125 mL
¼	cup granulated sugar	50 mL
1	tsp. dried dillweed*	5 mL

These Scandinavian-style cucumbers are very good for a smorgasbord.

1. Slice cucumbers very thin. Place in shallow glass dish and sprinkle with salt. Let stand at room temperature for about 30 minutes to draw out moisture.

2. Drain off accumulated liquid. Add vinegar, sugar, and dillweed. Cover and refrigerate for at least 4 hours.

* If available, use 1 Tbsp./15 mL chopped fresh dill. As is true with all herbs, fresh is best!

FANCIFUL SPINACH SALAD

Serves: 4

With everything prepared ahead, it's easy to assemble this tasty salad at a moment's notice.

1	lrg. bunch young spinach	1
12	sm. cherry tomatoes	12
	Dressing:	
⅓	cup good olive oil	75 mL
2	Tbs. red wine vinegar	25 mL
1	tsp. Dijon mustard	5 mL
1	clove garlic, crushed	1
¼	tsp. salt (or to taste)	1 mL
¼	tsp. pepper	1 mL
	Garnish:	
1	hard-cooked egg, sieved	1
2	Tbs. pine nuts, toasted	25 mL

1. Remove stems from spinach and save back for other purposes. Rinse leaves thoroughly and pat dry. Chill. Wash and stem tomatoes. Pat dry.

2. In screw-lid jar, combine all dressing ingredients. Shake well to blend. Let stand at least 20 minutes. Shake again before using.

3. Shortly before serving time, tear spinach leaves into bite-size pieces. Place in wide shallow serving bowl along with tomatoes. Drizzle with just enough dressing to coat (not drench) spinach and tomatoes. Toss lightly.

4. Sprinkle top of salad with sieved egg and toasted pine nuts. Serve immediately.

RUBY RED GRAPEFRUIT and RED ONION SALAD

Serves: 4-6

A very special salad.

2	med. ruby-red grapefruit	2
1	med. red onion, thinly sliced rings	1
1	lrg. bunch watercress, sprigs only*	1
	Dressing:	
⅓	cup salad oil	75 mL
2	Tbs. cider vinegar	25 mL
2	Tbs. heavy cream	25 mL
1	Tbs. fresh lemon juice	15 mL
1	tsp. granulated sugar	5 mL
½	tsp. salt (or to taste)	2 mL

1. With a sharp knife, skin the grapefruit. Separate each fruit segment from the membrane. Remove seeds. Keep chilled. Drain well before using. Watercress leaves should be patted dry with towel.
2. An hour or two before your guests arrive, arrange the fruit segments and onion rings with watercress interspersed in between on a large platter. Wrap and keep chilled.
3. Combine dressing ingredients in screw-lid jar. Shake well to blend. Let stand for a short while. At serving time, spoon or lightly drizzle over salad. Do not toss as this is a composed salad. Serve immediately.

* Use butter lettuce leaves to line plate if watercress is unavailable.

TOMATOES with DILL CREAM DRESSING

Serves: 4-6

One of our summertime favourites. Serve it with lamb or baron of beef.

6	med. tomatoes, sliced	6
	Dressing:	
¼	cup mayonnaise	50 mL
¼	cup dairy sour cream	50 mL
2	Tbs. red wine vinegar	25 mL
1	tsp. granulated sugar	5 mL
1	Tbs. chopped fresh dill	15 mL
¼	tsp. salt (or to taste)	1 mL
	Garnish:	
¼	cup diced cucumber	50 mL
1	Tbs. minced parsley	15 mL

1. Arrange sliced tomatoes slightly overlapping on serving platter.
2. In small mixing bowl, combine all dressing ingredients, mixing well. May be made ahead and kept refrigerated, but do not dress tomatoes until closer to serving time.
3. Just before serving time, spoon dressing over tomatoes. Sprinkle with diced cucumbers and minced parsley.

SAUERKRAUT MINGLE

Chill: 12-24 hrs.
Serves: 4-6

2	cups sauerkraut, drained	500 mL
¼	cup granulated sugar	50 mL
2	Tbs. white vinegar	25 mL
1	med. rib celery, chopped	1
1	sm. green pepper, chopped	1
1	sm. mild onion, chopped	1
1	Tbs. minced parsley	15 mL

Drain sauerkraut in colander and rinse lightly. Place in glass mixing bowl. Combine with remaining ingredients, mixing well. Cover and chill overnight. Will keep for several days.

The easiest salad in the book. And a very popular one, too. After a day or two of marinating, it surprisingly takes on a crunchy texture and an un-sauerkraut identity. Delicious with anything barbecued.

TABBOULI

Serves: 6

This tasty appetizer salad is a Middle-Eastern specialty that we love for the outdoors. It's very attractive served over a bed of lettuce with romaine or endive petals for scooping. For an interesting variation, add drained chickpeas or diced seedless cucumber.

1	cup fine bulgar (cracked wheat)	250 mL
3	med. tomatoes, chopped	3
2	med. green onions, chopped	2
2	med. bunches parsley, chopped	2
1	med. sweet onion, chopped	1
½	cup chopped fresh mint leaves	125 mL
	Dressing:	
6	Tbs. good olive oil	100 mL
4	Tbs. fresh lemon juice	50 mL
1	tsp. salt (or to taste)	5 mL
¼	tsp. freshly-ground pepper	1 mL

1. Wash bulgar. Then cover with boiling water and let soak for about 1 hour until tender. Drain and squeeze dry with hands. Place in mixing bowl with chopped vegetables and herbs.

2. Combine dressing ingredients and add to bulgar mixture, tossing lightly to mix. Taste for seasonings. May be made ahead. Tabbouli is best served at room temperature.

SHRIMP and TILSIT SALAD

Serves: 4-6

Tilsit is a nutty-textured cheese of German origin. Should it be unavailable, use its Danish counterpart, Havarti. This is a main course salad, but also makes a refreshing addition to an Oktoberfest celebration.

1	med. romaine lettuce	1
½	med. cucumber, diced	½
1	cup cubed Tilsit cheese	250 mL
½	lb. fresh baby shrimp	250 g
	Dressing:	
⅓	cup good olive oil	75 mL
2	Tbs. fresh lemon juice	25 mL
1	clove garlic, crushed	1
½	tsp. dried dillweed	2 mL
½	tsp. salt	2 mL
¼	tsp. dry mustard	1 mL
¼	tsp. pepper	1 mL

1. Wash and dry lettuce. Tear into bite-size pieces. Chill in plastic bag. Have remaining salad ingredients prepared.
2. Combine dressing in screw-lid jar. Shake well to blend. Let stand at room temperature for at least 20 minutes. Shake again before using.
3. Shortly before serving time, place lettuce in large shallow serving bowl. Sprinkle cucumbers, cheese, and shrimp on top. Drizzle with dressing, tossing lightly to coat all pieces. Serve immediately.

SNOW PEA-BABY CORN SALAD

Serves: 4-6

A very striking presentation. Pat vegetables dry with towel so that the dressing won't become diluted.

½	lb. fresh snow peas	250 g
	Boiling water-Pinch sugar	
1	tin baby corn	398 mL
1	doz. sm. cherry tomatoes	12
	Dressing:	
3	Tbs. fresh lemon juice	50 mL
1	lrg. egg yolk	1
1½	tsp. Dijon mustard	7 mL
½	tsp. dried dillweed	2 mL
½	tsp. salt (or to taste)	2 mL
9	Tbs. salad oil	135 mL

1. Snip off end tips of snow peas. In a wide skillet with boiling water and pinch sugar, cook snow peas until crisp-tender, about 2 minutes. Immediately drain and run under cold water to cool. Pat very dry.

2. Rinse baby corn and pat dry. Arrange snow peas, baby corn, and cherry tomatoes on a serving platter. Wrap and chill.

3. Dressing: Combine lemon juice, egg yolk, mustard, dillweed, and salt (to taste) in blender container. With machine running, add oil in a thin, steady stream until emulsified or thickened.

4. Just before serving time, lightly spoon or drizzle dressing over vegetables. No need to toss.

NOTE: Dressing may be made without blender. Simply combine lemon juice, yolk, mustard, dillweed, and salt in a heavy mixing bowl. Whisk in the oil, in a thin stream until smooth and well blended.

KIWI-STRAWBERRY SALAD

Serves: 4

The sweet-tart dressing in this salad adds a complementary lift to crisp greens, kiwifruit, and berries in season. Chopped macadamia nuts, an optional ingredient gives the whole presentation a rather exotic touch. For variation, try kiwi and cubed fresh pineapple, or kiwi and peeled orange segments.

1	sm. Romaine lettuce	1
2	med. kiwifruit	2
1	cup fresh strawberries	250 mL
	Dressing:	
6	Tbs. vegetable oil	90 mL
2	Tbs. cider vinegar	25 mL
1	Tbs. fresh lemon juice	15 mL
1	Tbs. liquid or soft honey	15 mL
1	Tbs. granulated sugar	15 mL
¼	tsp. salt (or to taste)	1 mL
1	Tbs. macadamia nut bits (opt.)	15 mL

1. Prepare dressing first. In a screw-lid jar, combine oil, vinegar, lemon juice, honey, sugar, and salt. Shake well to blend. Let stand for at least 20 minutes. Just before using, add chopped macadamias. Shake well.

2. Wash and pat lettuce leaves dry. Tear into bite-size pieces and place in large mixing bowl. Peel and slice kiwifruit. Hull and pat berries dry; halve if large. Set fruit aside.

3. At serving time, drizzle dressing over greens. Toss. Add fruit and mix lightly. Arrange on individual serving platters and serve immediately.

GREEK COUNTRY SALAD

Serves: 4

Typical of most Greek salads, this one features brine-cured calamatas (olives) and the distinctive salty Feta cheese. It's really easy to make and very lovely to look at. Delicious served with roast lamb or skewered meats.

4	med. tomatoes	4
1	med. green pepper	1
1	sm. mild onion	1
½	med. cucumber	½
Dressing:		
⅓	cup good olive oil	75 mL
2	Tbs. fresh lemon juice	25 mL
1	clove garlic, crushed	1
½	tsp. dried oregano leaves	2 mL
½	tsp. dried basil leaves	2 mL
½	tsp. salt (or to taste)	2 mL
¼	tsp. cracked pepper	1 mL
Garnish:		
12	calamatas (Greek olives)	12
4	oz. feta cheese, crumbled	125 g
6	anchovy fillets, chopped	6
1	Tbs. minced parsley	15 mL

1. Cut tomatoes, green pepper, onion, and cucumber into bite-size chunks. Place in a shallow serving bowl. Cover and keep chilled until serving time.
2. Whisk dressing ingredients together or shake well to blend in screw-lid jar. Let stand for at least 20 minutes at room temperature before using.
3. Spoon over salad, tossing lightly to mix. Garnish with calamatas, feta, anchovies (opt.), and minced parsley.

HOT POTATO SALAD

Serves: 6

The sweet-tangy flavour of this Bavarian-style potato salad makes a handsome addition to a backyard barbeque menu. Delicious with grilled frankfurters or smoked bratwurst.

¼	lb. bacon	
6	med. potatoes	6
2	lrg. eggs, hard-cooked (opt.)	2
¼	lb. bacon, 5-6 slices	125 g
1	sm. onion, chopped	1
2	Tbs. granulated sugar	25 mL
2	Tbs. all-purpose flour	25 mL
1	tsp. salt	5 mL
½	tsp. celery seed	2 mL
1	cup water	250 mL
½	cup regular white vinegar	125 mL
	Minced parsley	

1. Boil potatoes in skins until tender. Peel, slice, and keep warm. Shell eggs and slice. Set aside.

2. In a wide, stainless skillet, cook bacon slices until golden-crisp. Remove with slotted spatula, reserving pan drippings. Crumble or chop bacon and set aside.

3. Heat pan drippings, about ¼ cup/50 mL and in it, gently saute onion. Stir in sugar and then the flour, salt, and celery seed. Cook 2-3 minutes.

4. Add water and vinegar, cooking and stirring constantly until smooth and bubbly. Lightly mix in potatoes and eggs without breaking up the slices too much. Sprinkle with parsley and serve warm, straight from the pan.

HOT CHEVRE over SALAD GREENS

Serves: 4

Rounds or wedges of fresh goat cheese are left to marinate in olive oil scented with garlic and fresh basil leaves. The cheese is then coated with bread crumbs, baked, and then served over crisp salad greens. A most unusual and exciting presentation.

	Romaine and watercress	
	Chevre:	
4	thick slices chevre	4
½	cup good olive oil	125 mL
6	basil leaves, chopped	6
1	clove garlic, minced	1
	Freshly ground pepper	
⅓	cup fine bread crumbs	75 mL
	Dressing:	
6	Tbs. reserved olive oil	100 mL
2	Tbs. red wine vinegar	25 mL
1	clove garlic, crushed	1
½	tsp. Dijon mustard	2 mL
½	tsp. salt (or to taste)	2 mL

1. Rinse greens and pat dry. Tear lettuce into bite-size pieces and separate sprigs of watercress from coarse stems (save for soup). May be done ahead, but store in plastic bag to chill.
2. Cut chevre into 1 in./2.5 cm thick slices. Place on glass pie plate and pour olive oil over to coat. Sprinkle with basil, garlic, and freshly ground pepper. Let stand for at least 1 hour, basting with oil occasionally.
3. Remove chevre from marinade (reserve oil for dressing). Coat cheese with crumbs and place on small baking sheet.
4. Prepare vinaigrette by combining dressing ingredients in screw-lid jar and shaking vigorously to blend. Let stand for at least 20 minutes. Shake again before using.
5. At serving time, preheat oven to 450F/230C. Bake cheese for about 10 minutes or until soft and golden. Meanwhile toss romaine and watercress sprigs with dressing; portion among four platters. Top each serving with piece of hot cheese. Serve immediately.

MACARONI SALAD

Chill: 1 hr.
Serves: 4-6

Here's a good basic recipe that may be varied by replacing the grated carrot with fresh tiny shrimps or diced cheddar cheese. A touch of green pepper adds a winsome touch to this all 'round favourite.

2	cups elbow macaroni	500 mL
	Boiling water-Salt	
	Dressing:	
1	cup dairy sour cream	250 mL
½	cup mayonnaise	125 mL
2	Tbs. white vinegar	25 mL
1	tsp. granulated sugar	5 mL
½	tsp. dry mustard	2 mL
½	tsp. salt (or to taste)	2 mL
¼	tsp. pepper	1 mL
	Extras:	
1	med. carrot, grated	1
1	lrg. rib celery, diced	1
2	Tbs. minced parsley	25 mL

1. Cook macaroni in large pot of boiling salted water until al dente (tender, but firm). Place in colander and rinse under cold running water. Let stand to drain completely.
2. Meanwhile, combine all dressing ingredients in large mixing bowl. Add drained macaroni, carrot, celery, and parsley. Cover and let chill in refrigerator until serving time.

OVERNIGHT LAYERED SALAD

Chill: 12 hrs.
Serves: 8-10

An amazing salad! Even though it's prepared the night before, all the greens retain their colour and crispness. Ideal for any large gathering.

1	med. iceberg lettuce, shredded	1
1	med. sweet red onion, chopped	1
3	med. ribs celery, thinly sliced	3
1	lrg. green pepper, sliced	1
1½	cups frozen peas, semi-thawed	375 mL
	Dressing:	
1	cup good mayonnaise	250 mL
1	Tbs. wine vinegar	15 mL
2	tsp. granulated sugar	10 mL
1	tsp. seasoned salt	5 mL
¼	tsp. garlic powder (opt.)	1 mL
½	cup grated Parmesan (to top)	125 mL
	Garnish:	
2	lrg. hard-cooked eggs, in wedges	2
2	med. tomatoes, in wedges	2
8	med. pitted ripe olives, halved	8
4	Tbs. minced parsley	60 mL

1. If possible, use a large, straight-sided glass bowl to show off the layers. Begin with lettuce at the bottom, then onions, next celery, green pepper, and lastly peas.

2. In a small bowl, combine mayonnaise with vinegar, sugar, salt, and garlic powder. Spread over top of salad. Sprinkle with Parmesan. Cover tightly with foil. Refrigerate at least 12 hours and up to 24 hours.

3. Just before serving, arrange eggs, tomatoes, and olives on top. Sprinkle with parsley. Serve without tossing. Simply dig through layers with salad lifters..

MOZZARELLA and TOMATO SALAD

Marinate: 30 min.
Serves: 4-6

In this salad, a fresh basil dressing pleasantly complements both the cheese (plain or smoked) and tomatoes. It will not wilt or spoil easily and therefore makes an excellent dish for picnicking or patio dining. Try it with your favourite pasta creation.

4	med. tomatoes, sliced	4
½	lb. mozzarella, thinly sliced	250 g
	Dressing:	
¼	cup basil leaves, packed	50 mL
⅓	cup good olive oil	75 mL
2	Tbs. wine vinegar	25 mL
1	clove garlic, crushed	1
¼	tsp. salt (or to taste)	1 mL
¼	tsp. pepper	1 mL

1. On a serving platter, arrange the tomato slices alternately with the cheese, slightly overlapping them.

2. Finely mince the basil leaves. Place in screw-lid jar with olive oil, vinegar, garlic, and salt and pepper to taste. Shake well to blend.

3. Drizzle dressing over the salad. Cover and let marinate at room temperature for at least 30 minutes.

ROASTED PEPPER SALAD

Serves: 4

This Mediterranean-inspired salad is a superb accompaniment to lamb-on-the-spit, barbecued chicken, or steak over the coals. I like to use a combination of colours here: red, yellow, and green. The red and yellow peppers tend to be "pricey", but are much sweeter in flavour than the green. Well worth it! Like many Mediterranean salads, this one is best served at room temperature.

3	lrg. bell peppers	3
	Dressing:	
3	Tbs. olive oil	50 mL
1½	Tbs. red wine vinegar	25 mL
1	clove garlic, crushed	1
½	tsp. salt	2 mL
¼	tsp. pepper	1 mL
	Pinch granulated sugar	
	Garnish:	
2	Tbs. minced parsley	25 mL

1. Wash peppers and pat dry. Leave whole. Char over open flame or place them on baking sheet under broiler, about 4 in./10 cm from heat. Roast, turning with tongs until skin is blistered and tinged with brown (will take about 15 minutes).
2. Enclose peppers in paper bag to "sweat" for 15-20 minutes. Run (one at a time) under cold water, slipping off skins. Remove stem-ends and seeds. Cut peppers lengthwise into wide strips. Place on towelling to drain.
3. Combine dressing ingredients in screw-lid jar, shaking well to blend. Let stand at least 20 minutes.
4. Transfer peppers to small glass dish. Drizzle with dressing. Toss lightly. Sprinkle with parsley and let stand at room temperature for 1-2 hours.

BEET and PEAR SALAD

Serves: 4

2	med. beets, cooked, cooled*	2
1	med. butter lettuce	1
2	sm. firm, but ripe pears	2
	Dressing:	
6	Tbs. salad oil	75 mL
2	Tbs. red wine vinegar	25 mL
1	Tbs. minced shallots	15 mL
1	tsp. Dijon mustard	5 mL
½	tsp. salt	2 mL
¼	tsp. freshly-ground pepper	1 mL
⅛	tsp. granulated sugar	1 mL

Perfect for autumn and the festive season. This is a beautiful composed salad with no tossing required. However, the assembly is last minute, but should require no more than five minutes to piece together. We particularly like this accompanied with slices of country pate and crusty French bread. May also be made into individual salads.

1. Cut beets into julienne (match-like) strips. Wrap and set aside. Wash and separate leaves from lettuce. Pat dry and chill, leaving them whole. Wash pears, but do not slice until last minute.

2. Combine all dressing ingredients in screw-lid jar and shake well to blend. Let stand at least 20 minutes. Shake once more before using.

3. To arrange salad, line a large platter with the lettuce leaves. Without peeling, cut each pear into quarters and core. Slice into thin wedges and place in centre with a "nest" for the beets.

4. Add beets. Bring the salad to table and spoon or lightly drizzle dressing over all without drowning everything. Do not toss. Serve immediately.

* You may use tinned beets, but they will not have the nice flavour and crunchy texture of the freshly prepared. Drain thoroughly. Instructions for cooking beets from scratch appear in vegetable section.

GLORIFIED POTATO JACKETS

Serves: 2-4

A close look at the potato reveals that the outside is as interesting as the inside. Did you know that its leathery covering is a repository of nutrients — vitamins B, C, and G, plus many minerals, and even some high class protein? Teamed with grated cheddar, green onions, a bit of crumbled bacon, or whatever happens to cross your mind, potato skins have suddenly become the rage even in today's most sophisticated eateries. The problem lies in what to do with the pulp, and not the peel. Some solutions are offered below.

- Scrub 5 large baking potatoes (preferably the more mealy-textured russets or gems). Prick each with fork. Do not wrap in foil, so that the skin remains crisp. Bake in preheated 450F/230C oven for 45-55 minutes until potatoes feel soft when gently squeezed.
- Let potatoes cool slightly. Cut each in half lengthwise. Scoop out flesh, leaving ¼ in./1 cm thick shell. Save pulp for other purposes.
- Generously brush insides with melted butter or margarine. Sprinkle with grated cheddar and crumbled, cooked bacon bits. Set on baking sheet and briefly broil or bake at 450F/230C for 10 minutes until cheese is bubbly.
- If desired, top baked skins with sour cream and a sprinkling of chopped green onions. Also excellent with a spoonful or two of freshly-made salsa. Eat with fingers.

PULPY SOLUTIONS: If you like whipped potatoes, then mash the pulp while it is still hot. Once the potatoes turn cold, they lose their mealiness, and therefore their fluffiness. Cold potato pulp is excellent added to soups (as a thickener), to omelettes or frittatas, and to salads. We also like them pan-fried, like pancakes.

DO-AHEAD WHIPPED POTATOES

Oven: 350F/180C
Bake: 30 min.
Serves: 4-6

Whipped potatoes are a sure-fire winner with roasts or stews, but at their best only when piping hot. This one is a "make-ahead" with cream cheese and dairy sour cream to keep it moist and smooth. Netted gems, Russets, or Idahos are best for mashing since they have a dry, mealy texture.

6	lrg. potatoes, peeled	6
	Boiling water	
1	sm. pkg. cream cheese	125 g
½	cup dairy sour cream	125 mL
½	tsp. salt or to taste	2 mL
¼	tsp. pepper	1 mL
	Topping:	
3	Tbs. butter, melted	50 mL
2	green onions, minced	2
½	cup dry bread crumbs	125 mL

1. Cook potatoes, covered in large saucepan with boiling water. Potatoes should be very tender. Drain thoroughly, saving cooking liquid for gravy or soup.
2. Mash potatoes or whip with mixer until smooth. Add cream cheese, sour cream, and seasonings to taste. Beat until light and fluffy. Spoon into well-buttered casserole. May be made ahead up to this point.
3. Combine topping mixture and sprinkle over potatoes. Bake in preheated oven, uncovered until heated through, about 30 minutes.

POTATO LATKES

Yields: 10-12

Potato Latkes make an excellent accompaniment to any pot roast or stew. They are best eaten as they are cooked. Delicious served with dairy sour cream or homemade applesauce.

6	med. baking potatoes	6
1	sm. onion, finely minced	1
2	lrg. eggs, slightly beaten	2
¼	cup all-purpose flour	50 mL
¾	tsp. salt	5 mL
	Vegetable oil for cooking	

1. Peel and then grate potatoes on coarse shredder. Drain off liquid and squeeze potatoes dry in a tea towel. Place in a mixing bowl with onion, eggs, flour, and salt. Mix well.

2. Heat thin layer of oil in a large skillet until very hot. Drop batter by scant ¼ cupsful/50 mL. Cook only a few at a time, slightly flattening each with a wide spatula.

3. Fry 2-3 minutes per side or until crisp and golden-brown. Drain on paper towelling and serve immediately.

POTATOES BOULANGERE

Oven: 400F/200C
Bake: 40-50 min.
Serves: 4

Gems or russets are best for this flavourful potato delight. Excellent with all meats.

5	lrg. potatoes	5
4	Tbs. butter or margarine	60 mL
1	med. onion, thinly sliced	1
1	lrg. clove garlic, minced	1
1	tin chicken or beef broth	284 mL
	Salt and freshly-ground pepper	
	Butter or margarine	

1. Preheat oven. Peel and thinly slice potatoes crosswise. Cover and set aside briefly.

2. In a heavy ovenproof skillet or small roaster, melt the butter and slowly cook onion and garlic, about 10 minutes.

3. Add sliced potatoes and undiluted broth, mixing well. Let come to a boil. Cover and immediately transfer to oven to bake for 20 minutes.

4. Uncover and sprinkle with a little salt and lots of freshly-ground pepper. Dot with bits of butter. Continue baking uncovered for another 20 minutes or until potatoes are golden and fork-tender.

ORANGE-GINGER CARROTS

Serves: 4

Did you know that carrots contain more natural sugar than any other vegetable aside from the sugar beet? Strangely though, the calories in a medium-size carrot amount to less than a package of sugarless gum, about 30.

6	med. carrots, scraped	6
	Boiling water-Pinch sugar	
	Sauce:	
1	Tbs. granulated sugar	15 mL
2	tsp. grated orange rind	10 mL
¼	cup fresh orange juice	50 mL
1	tsp. cornstarch	5 mL
¼	tsp. powdered ginger	1 mL
¼	tsp. salt	1 mL
	Extras:	
2	Tbs. butter or margarine	25 mL
1	Tbs. chopped mint or parsley	15 mL

1. Halve carrots lengthwise. Cook in small amount of boiling water in a wide skillet with pinch of sugar added until crisp-tender, about 15 minutes. Drain well.

2. In a small saucepan, combine the sauce ingredients. Cook over medium heat, stirring constantly until thick and bubbly. Immediately remove from heat and add butter.

3. Pour over carrots and let them warm through under gentle heat. Do not let boil. Sprinkle with mint or parsley before serving.

RUTABAGA PUFF

Oven: 350F/180C
Bake: 30 min.
Serves: 6

What most people consider as yellow turnip is really rutabaga. Look for the small or medium-size ones as the monstrosities tend to be pithy and sometimes spongy. Mashed rutabaga makes a superb companion for that Thanksgiving or Christmas Day turkey. Edie, my mom-in-law never let a festive occasion go by without this one.

6	cups cubed, peeled rutabaga	1.5 L
	Boiling water — Pinch sugar	
2	Tbs. butter or margarine	25 mL
2	lrg. eggs	2
3	Tbs. all-purpose flour	50 mL
1	Tbs. brown sugar	15 mL
1	tsp. baking powder	5 mL
½	tsp. salt (or to taste)	2 mL
¼	tsp. pepper	1 mL
	Topping:	
½	cup fine dry bread crumbs	125 mL
2	Tbs. butter, melted	25 mL

1. Cook rutabaga in small amount of boiling water with pinch of sugar added. When fork-tender, drain thoroughly.
2. Mash or whip. Mix in butter and eggs, beating until well blended. Combine flour, brown sugar, baking powder, salt and pepper to taste. Add to rutabaga mixture.
3. Spoon into well-buttered 1½ qt./1.5 L casserole or baking dish. Top with mixture of fine crumbs and melted butter.
4. Preheat oven and bake until puffed and golden-brown, about 30 minutes. Serve piping hot.

STUFFED TOMATOES PROVENCALE

Oven: 425F/220C
Bake: 10 min.
Serves: 4

4	med. firm, but ripe tomatoes	4
	Salt	
2	Tbs. olive oil	25 mL
1	sm. onion, chopped	1
1	med. shallot, minced	1
¼	cup dry bread crumbs	50 mL
2	Tbs. minced parsley	25 mL

1. Slice off top third of each tomato. Reserve tops. Scoop out all seeds and water, but leave pulp. Lightly sprinkle insides of each tomato bottom with salt and invert to drain for about 10 minutes. Chop up "tops" and drain well.

2. In medium saucepan, heat oil until hot. Add onion and shallot, cooking and stirring until tender, about 5 minutes. Add chopped tomato bits. Cook until most of the liquid has evaporated.

3. Remove from heat. Stir in the crumbs and parsley. Stuff hollows of tomato bottoms with mixture. Bake in preheated 425F/220C oven for about 10 minutes or just until heated through. Tomatoes should hold their shape. Do not overbake. Serve hot.

Provencale refers to foods cooked in the style of Provence (a region in southern France). A liberal amount of garlic, parsley, mushrooms or tomatoes, and oil is used. In this case, try a little chopped green pepper or ripe olives for variation. Toasted pine nuts sprinkled on top are nice, too. Good with roasts or grilled meats.

STIR-FRIED BROCCOLI and FRIENDS

Stir-fry: 3-5 min.
Serves: 4

1	lb. broccoli, washed	500 g
2	Tbs. corn or peanut oil	25 mL
1	med. clove garlic, crushed	1
½	tsp. salt	2 mL
⅓	cup light broth or water	75 mL
1	Tbs. good soy sauce	15 mL
½	tsp. granulated sugar	2 mL

1. Peel or scrape off the tough outer layer from the stems of broccoli. Divide flower part into small florets and slice stems on the diagonal, about ¼ in./0.5 cm thick.
2. Heat wok or heavy skillet (cast iron) until hot. Use medium-high setting. Add oil and when rippling hot, add garlic and salt, quickly stirring for a few seconds without burning garlic.
3. Add broccoli. Toss and flip to coat with hot oil. Lower heat to medium. Stir in soy, broth, and sugar. Cover and let vegetables steam for 3-5 minutes.
4. Broccoli should emerge crisp-tender in texture and a vibrant green in colour. Serve piping hot.

Try:
- Broccoli and Cauliflower Florets
- Broccoli and Thinly Sliced Carrots
- Broccoli and Sliced Bamboo Shoots
- Broccoli and Sliced Kohlrabi

A good stir-fry requires: (1) high heat, (2) constant flipping and tossing, and (3) quick cooking so that the vegetables remain tender and crisp and vibrant in colour.

ZUCCHINI BOATS

Oven: 350F/180C
Bake: 40-45 min.
Serves: 4

This member of the squash family is otherwise known as "zucchine" to the Italians; "courgette" to the French; and "young marrow" to the English. Try it stuffed. Delicious!

2	med. zucchini, 6 in./15 cm	2
	Boiling water-Pinch sugar	
	Stuffing:	
2	Tbs. butter or margarine	25 mL
1	sm. onion, finely chopped	1
2	Tbs. minced parsley	25 mL
2	cups soft bread bits	500 mL
1	lrg. egg, lightly beaten	1
4	Tbs. freshly-grated Parmesan	60 mL
½	tsp. salt (or to taste)	2 mL
	Topping:	
	Freshly-grated Parmesan	

1. Trim off ends of zucchini. Leave whole and do not peel. Cook for 5 minutes in boiling water (to cover) with pinch sugar added. Drain and immediately refresh under cold water.
2. Halve each zucchini lengthwise. Scrape out soft pulp with spoon and chop fine. Save shells for stuffing.
3. In a medium pan, melt butter and gently saute onion until tender. Add chopped zucchini and parsley.
4. Remove from heat and add soft crumbs, egg, Parmesan, and salt to taste. Mix lightly, but thoroughly.
5. Fill zucchini shells. Place in a shallow baking dish. Sprinkle with extra Parmesan and bake in preheated oven, uncovered for about 40 minutes or until heated through.

RED CABBAGE with APPLES

Braise: 1½ hrs.
Serves: 6 or more

Make this German favourite the day before to let all the flavours meld. Simply reheat and serve. Delicious with roasts and stuffed meats such as rouladen.

2	lb. head red cabbage	1 kg
2	Tbs. butter or margarine	25 mL
2	Tbs. granulated sugar	25 mL
1	med. onion, chopped	1
2	med. apples, peeled, sliced	2
⅔	cup red wine vinegar	150 mL
1	cup hot water (maybe more)	250 mL
1½	tsp. salt	7 mL
¼	tsp. nutmeg	1 mL
3	Tbs. red currant jelly	50 mL

1. Trim and core cabbage. Shred into fine strips with knife (do not use grater). Set aside.
2. In large, wide skillet, melt butter. Add sugar and slowly saute over low heat until caramel-coloured (watch carefully).
3. Mix in onions and apples. Cover. Cook, stirring until mixture is lightly browned, about 3 minutes. Stir in cabbage. Add vinegar, mixing well. Cover and cook slowly for 10 minutes.
4. Add water, salt, and nutmeg. Let come to a boil. Reduce heat to low. Cover and let braise for about 1½ hours until cabbage is tender and most of the liquid has dissipated. May be made ahead up to this point, but reheat.
5. Just before serving, stir in currant jelly. Taste for seasonings and serve while hot.

* Braise means to cook slowly in a small amount of liquid in a covered pan.

SPINACH with BACON, RAISINS, and PINE NUTS

Serves: 4

This side dish pairs well with just about any lamb dish.

1	lb. fresh young spinach	500 g
2	thick slices bacon	2
1	tsp. vegetable oil	5 mL
¼	cup golden raisins	50 mL
3	Tbs. pine nuts	50 mL

1. Wash spinach thoroughly. Dice bacon.
2. In a wide skillet, heat oil and cook bacon slices until golden-brown. Remove and drain on paper towelling; then chop. Reserve oil in pan.
3. Shortly before serving time, heat oil in pan. Add raisins and pine nuts, sauteing gently until raisins are plumped and pine nuts are golden. Remove with slotted spatula and set aside.
4. Add spinach leaves. Stir and cook until tender, but still a bright green. When most of the liquid has evaporated, add bacon, raisins, and pine nuts. Serve immediately.

ASPARAGUS with PISTACHIOS

Serves: 4

The pistachio, a nut belonging to the cashew family is a native of western Asia and southern Europe. Its greenish-yellow kernel adds a delightful touch to freshly-cooked asparagus.

1½	lbs. fresh asparagus	750 g
	Boiling water - Pinch sugar	
⅓	cup butter or margarine	75 mL
⅓	cup pistachios, chopped	75 mL
1	Tbs. fresh lemon juice	15 mL
1	Tbs. minced fresh herbs	15 mL

1. Snap off tough asparagus bottoms or if stalks are thick, scrape off woody layer with a swivel peeler. Trim and wash.
2. Place asparagus in a wide skillet with boiling water to cover. Sprinkle in a pinch of sugar. Cook until tender-crisp and still a bright-green, about 5 minutes.
3. While asparagus are cooking, melt butter in a small saucepan. Add pistachios, lemon juice, and herbs, stirring until hot.
4. Drain asparagus and arrange on warm serving platter. Drizzle with hot buttered pistachios. Serve immediately.

SPUR-of-the-MOMENT PICKLED BEETS

Serves: 4-6

Rosey-red onions beautifully complement the deep, rich burgundy of freshly-prepared beets. Tinned ones may be used here, but you will miss out on the sweet, earthy flavour and the crunchy texture of the fresh.

3	cups sliced, cooked beets*	750 mL
1	med. onion, sliced	1
½	cup reserved beet juice	125 mL
½	cup cider vinegar	125 mL
⅓	cup granulated sugar	75 mL
¼	tsp. salt	1 mL

1. Layer beet and onion slices in heatproof serving bowl.
2. In a small saucepan (stainless), combine beet juice or water, cider vinegar, sugar, and salt. Heat, stirring over medium heat just long enough to dissolve sugar crystals.
3. Pour hot mixture over the beets and onions. Cool. Then refrigerate, covered for at least 4 hours before serving. Stir occasionally. Will keep a good one week under refrigeration.

* HOW TO PREPARE BEETS: Scrub 6 medium-size beets, leaving roots in tact and 1½ in./4 cm of the stems (to keep colour loss at a minimum). Do not peel. Place in large pot with cold water to cover. Bring to a boil. Cover and reduce heat. Let simmer gently until tender. Count on 30 minutes for medium beets. Drain off juices and save. Cool beets under cold water. Trim off stems and roots, and slip off skins. Now the beets are ready for slicing, dicing, or shredding. Use for salads, cakes and breads, or pickling (as above).

HERBED VEGETABLE KEBOBS

Grill: 15 min.

All vegetables on the same skewer should have similar cooking times. Parboil those which take longer eg. potatoes, squash, and corn. Baste to keep moist and add extra flavour.

	Tiny new potatoes, scrubbed	
	Thick rounds of zucchini	
	Large mushroom caps	
	Chunks of green or red pepper	
	Wedges of Spanish onion	
	Baste:	
¼	cup vegetable oil	50 mL
2	tsp. minced chives	10 mL
1	tsp. dried dillweed	5 mL
1	tsp. lemon pepper or salt	5 mL

1. Parboil small potatoes (unpeeled) for about 10 minutes; zucchini rounds for about 5 minutes. Cool. Mushroom caps, bell peppers and onion do not need to be pre-cooked. Thread vegetables onto skewers.

2. Combine baste ingredients in small saucepan and heat briefly. Set aside.

3. Grill vegetable kebobs about 6 in./14 cm from heat source, turning and brushing several times with baste. Cook until tender, about 15 minutes. Serve one skewer per person.

CARROT MARMALADE

(Yields: 4 jelly glasses)

2	cups sliced carrots	500 mL
2	med. lemons, for juice	2
1	lrg. orange, grated rind	1
3	cups granulated sugar	750 mL
½	bottle liquid pectin	½
	Sterilized jars and hot paraffin	

Whenever I bring out my marmalade, people can't believe that it's made from carrots. Then, they all want the recipe...not only because it's so unusual, but also because it sounds so healthy.

1. Cook carrot slices in small amount of water until tender. Drain well in colander. Then grind or finely chop (processor may be used) and place in a large saucepan.

2. Add lemon juice and orange rind. Remove outer white pith from orange and cut the "meat" into small chunks. Add to the carrot mixture. Mix in the sugar.

3. Place over high heat and let contents come to a full rolling boil (one that can't be stirred down). Boil hard for 1 minute, stirring all the while. Remove from heat.

4. Immediately add the pectin and keep stirring for 5 minutes to prevent floating fruit. Ladle into prepared jars. Cover with hot paraffin and seal with lids.

NOTE: The recipe may be doubled. Do not reduce the amount of sugar asked for, otherwise the marmalade may not set.

SOUPS

GARDEN HALIBUT SOUP

Serves: 4

A light-hearted main course soup. Serve it with warm croissants or fresh-from-the oven bread.

2	Tbs. butter or olive oil	25 mL
2	sm. leeks, white part, sliced	2
1	med. clove garlic, minced	1
1	qt. good chicken broth	1 L
2	med. carrots, quartered	2
1	med. rib celery, sliced	1
6	whole peppercorns	6
1	med. bay leaf	1
2	cups torn escarole or spinach	500 mL
2	sm. zucchini, sliced in rounds	2
	Salt, if necessary	
¾	lb. skinned, deboned halibut	350 g

1. Heat butter or oil in a large pot. Add sliced leeks and garlic, sauteing until tender.

2. Add broth, carrots, celery, peppercorns, and bay leaf. Bring to a boil. Reduce heat. Cover and let simmer for 15 minutes (may be done ahead).

3. To the hot broth, add torn escarole or spinach leaves and zucchini rounds. Simmer briefly uncovered, about 10 minutes. Season as necessary.

4. Cut halibut into chunks and place on top of soup. Spoon broth over and cook about 5 minutes or until fish turns opaque and firm. Do not overcook. Ladle into warm bowls.

SOME TURKEY SOUP

Serves: 6

Save back that turkey carcass and those leftover scraps for this fabulous-tasting soup. Nice served with homemade soda bread and a chunk of cheddar.

Broth:
Turkey carcass and leftovers

1	carrot, split lengthwise	1
1	rib celery with leaves	1
1	bay leaf	1
6	whole peppercorns	6

Extras:

2	med. leeks, white portion	2
2	Tbs. butter or margarine	25 mL
2	med. carrots, sliced thick	2
2	med. ribs celery, chopped	2
¼	cup pot barley or rice	50 mL
1	cup frozen peas (add last)	250 mL
2	Tbs. minced parsley	25 mL
	Salt and pepper to taste	

1. Pick off whatever meat there is on carcass and set aside. Break up carcass to fit stock pot. Cover with cold water. Add remaining broth items.

2. Bring to a boil, skimming off foam. Reduce heat to low. Cover and simmer gently for 2-3 hours. Strain, transferring liquid to another pot or if not using immediately, to a mason jar (refrigerate or freeze). Skim off fat — best done after broth has cooled off.

3. Split leeks lengthwise and rinse out grit under running water. Chop and saute in melted butter in above stock pot. Add broth, sliced carrots, chopped celery, and barley or rice. Simmer 1 hour or until barley is tender.

4. Shortly before serving time, add reserved turkey bits, the peas, parsley, and seasonings to taste. Ladle into warm bowls.

COUNTRY-STYLE SPLIT PEA SOUP

Serves: 4

1	cup dried split peas	250 mL
6	cups water	1.5 L
1	med. smoked pork hock	1
2	med. leeks (whites), chopped	2
1	med. onion, chopped	1
1	cup chopped celery leaves	250 mL
1	med. bay leaf	1
1	tsp. salt (or to taste)	5 mL
½	tsp. freshly ground pepper	2 mL
2	med. carrots, sliced	2
	Minced parsley for garnish	

1. Place peas in a large pot. Rinse and soak overnight in water to cover.
2. Next day, bring contents of pot to a boil and let simmer for 30 minutes. Add pork hock, ONLY 1 of the chopped leeks, all of the onion, celery leaves, bay leaf, and seasonings.
3. Bring to a boil. Cover and reduce heat. Let simmer over low heat for about 2 hours or until both meat and peas are tender.
4. Remove hock and set aside. Let mixture cool slightly. Mash or puree mixture until smooth. Return to pot. Add carrots and the other chopped leek. Cover. Let simmer gently until carrots are tender, about 20 minutes. Stir often.
5. Meanwhile, dice up meat from hock and add to soup. Taste for seasonings. Ladle into warm bowls. Sprinkle with minced parsley before serving.

Either green or yellow split peas can be used here. For the penny-wise, this soup ends up a winner. It's chockful of flavour and a lot of good things from the garden. Save back that ham bone (with some meat left on) and use it in place of the pork hock.

CORN KERNEL SOUP

Serves: 4

Some of the sweetest and best-tasting corn is harvested in the Chilliwack area, just outside of Vancouver. Scrape it fresh from the cob for this marvellous treat.

3	med. ears of corn	3
2	Tbs. butter or margarine	25 mL
1	med. onion, minced	1
1	lrg. shallot, minced	1
2	Tbs. all-purpose flour	25 mL
3	cups milk	750 mL
½	tsp. salt (or to taste)	2 mL
¼	tsp. pepper	1 mL
	Minced chives or parsley	

1. Husk corn. Using long, sharp knife, slice off strips of corn kernels, enough to make 2½ cups/625 mL. Set aside.
2. In a large saucepan, melt butter. Add onion and shallot, cooking until tender. Add flour, stirring until bubbly — about 3 minutes.
3. Add milk. Stir constantly over medium heat until mixture thickens slightly. May be made ahead up to this point, but reheat.
4. Lower heat. Add corn and simmer gently until kernels are tender and heated through, about 10 minutes. Do not let boil or overcook. Season to taste. Serve immediately with chives or parsley to garnish.

CORN-OYSTER SOUP: Add 8-12 freshly-shucked oysters and their juices at end of cooking. Heat only briefly — just until edges curl up.

CREAM of VEGETABLE SOUP

Serves: 4-6

2	cups finely chopped vegetables*	500 mL
3	Tbs. butter or margarine	50 mL
1	sm. onion, finely chopped	1
3	Tbs. all-purpose flour	50 mL
2	cups milk (or part cream)	500 mL
1	cup chicken stock or broth	250 mL
½	tsp. salt (or to taste)	2 mL
¼	tsp. freshly-ground pepper	1 mL
	Minced parsley or paprika	

1. Melt butter in a large saucepan. Add chopped onion and saute gently for about 5 minutes. Add chopped vegetables cooking with lid on, until tender.
2. Sprinkle in the flour and cook for an additional 3 minutes. Add both milk and broth, stirring constantly until well blended and slightly thickened. Do not let boil.
3. Salt and pepper to taste. Ladle into warm bowls, sprinkling each with a little minced parsley or paprika. Serve straight away.

* Use chopped up asparagus, broccoli, cauliflower, carrots, corn, sliced mushrooms or any combination of the forementioned.

Kirk Waldron is one of those young men who loves to cook. He impressed me with the cream of mushroom soup he made for his mom's Christmas dinner a couple of years back. Kirk's recipe is extremely versatile, delicious with everything from carrots to celery and broccoli.

COOL GAZPACHO

Chill: 4-6 hrs.
Serves: 6

A salad soup for those lazy, hazy days of summer. Good with croutons.

Base:

2	cups vegetable cocktail*	500 mL
2	Tbs. good olive oil	25 mL
3	Tbs. red wine vinegar	50 mL
1	Tbs. fresh lemon juice	15 mL
1	tsp. Worcestershire sauce	5 mL
1	tsp. granulated sugar	5 mL
½	tsp. salt (or to taste)	2 mL
¼	tsp. pepper	1 mL
¼	tsp. tabasco	1 mL

Garnish:

1	lrg. tomato, seeded, diced	1
½	cup chopped celery	125 mL
½	cup chopped green pepper	125 mL
½	cup chopped cucumber	125 mL
¼	cup chopped sweet onion	50 mL
1	med. clove garlic, minced	1
1	Tbs. minced green onion	15 mL
1	Tbs. minced parsley	15 mL

Combine ingredients for soup base (all to taste) in a large glass bowl. Add remaining vegetable garnishings. Stir well to mix. Chill thoroughly before serving.

* Vegetable cocktail juice is available in cans or bottles.

COCK-A-LEEKIE

Serves: 6

1	med. utility chicken	1.5 kg
2	qts. cold water	2 L
3	lrg. leeks, white portion	3
⅓	cup pot barley or rice	75 mL
	Salt and pepper to taste	
	Minced parsley to garnish	

This tasty chicken and leek soup is a Scottish tradition. In the days when cock fights were popular, the loser often times landed up in the soup pot. Prunes were sometimes added for extra flavour. Should you wish to do this, throw in 6-8 along with the leeks.

1. Segment chicken and place in soup pot with cold water to cover. Bring to a boil over high heat, skimming off any foam that forms (important for clear broth).
2. Reduce heat. Cover and let simmer about 1 hour until chicken is tender. A stewing chicken will take up to 2 hours.
3. Meanwhile, split leeks lengthwise and run under cold water to rinse out sand and grit. Chop.
4. Remove chicken pieces and set aside to cool slightly. Add chopped leeks and the barley to broth. Let simmer for 45 minutes or until barley is cooked.
5. Pick off meat from chicken, discarding skin and bones. Save back breast meat for sandwiches. Cut chicken into bite-size chunks and return to the soup. Simmer to heat through. Add salt and pepper to taste.
6. Ladle soup into heated bowls. Sprinkle with minced parsley.

BRANDIED PUMPKIN SOUP

Serves: 6

Pumpkin soup spiked with a little brandy makes a most welcome treat for the cooler autumn days. Made easy with tinned pumpkin.

1	med. onion, chopped	1
2	Tbs. butter or margarine	25 mL
3½	cups chicken broth	875 mL
1	med. tin pumpkin puree	398 mL
2	Tbs. brandy	25 mL
½	tsp. salt (or to taste)	2 mL
¼	tsp. pepper	1 mL
¼	tsp. nutmeg	1 mL
1	cup light cream	250 mL
	Chopped chives	
	Homemade croutons	

1. In a large saucepan, gently saute chopped onions in melted butter until tender, about 5 minutes. Add broth and bring to a boil. Reduce heat and cover. Simmer 10 minutes.

2. Add pumpkin, brandy, and seasonings (all to taste). Whisk or stir until smooth and well blended. Then simmer for another 10 minutes.

3. Just before serving time, add cream and simmer just until heated through. Do not let boil. Ladle into warm bowls and sprinkle with chopped chives. Serve with croutons.

CROUTONS: Cut day-old French or Italian bread into ½ in./1.5 cm cubes to make 2 cups/500 mL in total. Bake in preheated 275F/140C oven for 15 minutes. Remove and toss toasted cubes in ⅓ cup/75 mL melted butter or margarine (seasoned as desired with Parmesan, herbs, etc.). Coat as evenly as possible. Spread out on baking sheet and bake for 20-30 minutes until crisp and golden. Cool and store in jar.

"ACE-in-the-HOLE" CLAM CHOWDER

Serves: 4-6

From a super cook and gardener, Elin Langlois. It's her ace-in-the-hole when friends drop by unexpectedly. Serve with a loaf of crusty bread and a hefty chunk of cheese; and don't forget the chilled white wine!

4	oz. lean salt pork, diced*		125 g
1	tsp. cooking oil		5 mL
1	med. onion, chopped		1
1	med. rib celery, chopped		1
3	cups water		750 mL
4	cups raw cubed potatoes		1 L
2	tins whole baby clams	EA.	142 g
2	cups light cream		500 mL
½	tsp. thyme leaves, crumbled		2 mL
½	tsp. salt (or to taste)		2 mL
¼	tsp. pepper		1 mL

Extras:
Soft butter or margarine
Paprika or minced parsley

1. In large, heavy saucepan, brown salt pork in a little oil. Drain off excess fat, leaving thin film on bottom. Add onion and celery. Saute until tender and golden.
2. Add water and potatoes. Bring to a boil and then reduce heat to low. Simmer partially covered with lid until potatoes are tender, but not falling apart.
3. Add clams and its liquor (juices), the cream, thyme, and seasonings to taste. Remove from heat, if making ahead. Otherwise heat gently, but thoroughly. Do not let it boil.
4. Stir in 2 Tbs./25 mL butter or margarine. Ladle into warm soup bowls. Sprinkle each serving with paprika or minced parsley. Serve immediately.

* Or use 4 thick slices bacon.

AUTUMN BORSCHT

Simmer: 2 hrs.
Serves: 4-6

Borscht is a hearty peasant soup with many variations. Some cooks like to add diced potatoes; others, shredded cabbage or chopped up beet tops. This one has julienned strips of beets and carrots to brighten up a dull winter day.

4	short ribs with bones	4
6	cups cold water	1.5 L
2	med. beets, scrubbed	2
1	lrg. carrot, scraped	1
1	sm. onion	1
1	med. tin tomatoes	398 mL
1	sm. lemon, for juice	1
1	Tbs. granulated sugar	15 mL
½	tsp. salt	2 mL
¼	tsp. pepper	1 mL

Garnish:
Dairy sour cream
Fresh chopped dillweed

1. Place short ribs in large pot with water to cover. Bring to a boil and skim off any foam that appears on surface. Reduce heat to low simmer. Cover. Cook for 1 hour or until meat is very tender.

2. Remove ribs. If you wish a clear broth, strain through cheesecloth. Skim off fat. Cut beets, carrots, and onion into julienne strips (thin, match-like strips). Add to broth along with tomatoes, liquid included. Simmer on low heat, covered for another 1 hour or until vegetables are tender.

3. Add lemon juice, sugar, and salt and pepper to taste. If desired meat may be added. Heat through and ladle into warm soup bowls. Serve with sour cream and dillweed on the side.

BASIC CHICKEN STOCK

About: 6 cups/1.5 L

3	lb. chicken backs and necks	1.5 kg
2	qts. cold water	2 L
1	med. onion, quartered	1
1	rib celery with leaves	1
1	med. carrot, split lengthwise	1
6	whole peppercorns	6

For great tasting soups and sauces. May be frozen.

1. Place above ingredients in large stock pot. Bring to a boil. Skim off foam (important for clear broth). Reduce heat. Cover and let simmer about 2 hours.
2. Remove chicken bones. Strain into container and chill. Lift off fat. May be frozen. Do not season until added to recipe.

FRESHENING CANNED BROTH

Yields About: 2½ cups/625 mL

2	tins chicken or beef broth EA.	284 mL
1	med. onion, in quarters	1
1	med. carrot, split lengthwise	1
1	rib celery with leaves	1
3	sprigs parsley	3

Canned broth can be made more palatable with a little doctoring from the herbs and vegetables in your vegetable bin.

Without diluting the broth, add to large soup pot with everything else. Simmer, partially covered for about 30 minutes. Strain. Refrigerate or freeze.

PARSLEY PESTO for PASTA

Yields: 2 cups/500 mL

2	cups fresh parsley sprigs	500 mL
2	Tbs. dried basil leaves	25 mL
2	lrg. cloves garlic, minced	2
¼	cup chopped pine nuts	50 mL
1	tsp. salt	5 mL
½	tsp. freshly-ground pepper	2 mL
1	cup good olive oil	250 mL
½	cup freshly-grated Parmesan	125 mL

When fresh basil is out of season, try parsley pesto as an alternative for spiffying up your favourite pasta.

1. Remove and discard coarse stems from parsley. Chop up the sprigs and place in a mixing bowl with the dried basil. Using back of wooden spoon, mash until smooth and paste-like.

2. Work in garlic, pine nuts, salt and pepper. Then add the olive oil, incorporating a little at a time until well blended. At this point, the pesto may be made ahead and stored in the refrigerator.

3. Stir in Parmesan just before using. Thin out pesto with 3-4 Tbs./50 mL hot water from cooking pasta and toss lightly with hot, drained noodles.

BLENDER METHOD: Combine all ingredients except Parmesan in blender container. Whirl until smooth. Remove and stir in Parmesan.

PESTO with FRESH BASIL

Serves: 4-6

We can thank the basil-loving Italians for this simply suave emulsion. Traditionally, it's hand ground with a mortar and pestle, but with a little help from your blender or processor, the sauce can be prepared in a matter of minutes. Pesto keeps well in the refrigerator for a good week or more. It also freezes beautifully. Dab pesto over broiled steaks or fish; spoon it over steamed zucchini or fresh tomato slices. When mingled with bucatini (hollow rods of pasta), potatoes, and green beans, the dish then becomes an Italian favourite.

2	cups packed basil leaves	500 g
2	cloves garlic, minced	2
3	Tbs. pine nuts	50 mL
½	cup good olive oil	125 mL
1	tsp. salt	5 mL
½	cup freshly grated Parmesan	125 mL
2	Tbs. grated Romano cheese	25 mL
3	Tbs. soft butter or margarine	50 mL

1. Place basil leaves, garlic, pine nuts, olive oil, and salt in blender or processor. Whirl until a thick, smooth sauce forms. To freeze, note instructions below.
2. Transfer the sauce to a mixing bowl and beat in the cheeses and then the softened butter until well blended. The pesto may be refrigerated.
3. Before using pesto over pasta, thin out with 1-2 Tbs./15-25 mL hot pasta water.

FREEZING PESTO: For a fresher flavour, do not add the cheeses or butter. Divide into small containers and freeze. Thaw pesto overnight in refrigerator, then beat in cheeses and the butter.

RICE, STEAMED the EASY WAY

Simmer: 20 min.
Serves: 4-6

| 2 | cups raw long-grain rice | 500 mL |
| 3 | cups cold water | 750 mL |

1. Place rice in a heavy, medium-size saucepan with a tight fitting lid. Add lots of cold water and swish around with your hand to remove excess starch. Drain off as much water as possible. Repeat 2-3 times until water is clear.

2. Measure cold water and add to washed rice. Bring to a boil over medium-high heat and let it continue bubbling without stirring. When most of the water has dissipated and tiny craters appear on the surface, quickly pop on the lid.

3. Immediately reduce heat to the lowest possible setting and "steam" without lifting lid (important) for a full 20 minutes. Turn off heat and let rice stand for a few minutes (up to 30 minutes) before fluffing with fork. To keep it hot for a longer time, set the whole thing over a pan of hot water.

Served in the Oriental manner, steamed rice requires no butter or salt. It provides a neutral accompaniment to each seasoned dish. Rice is not as intimidating to cook as you may think. Try it. Remember that rice triples in volume when cooked.

BOUNTIFUL FRIED RICE

Serves: 4

4	cups cold, leftover cooked rice	1 L
2	lrg. eggs, lightly beaten	2
3	Tbs. corn or peanut oil	50 mL
1	cup diced cooked meat (opt.)*	250 mL
2	lrg. ribs celery, diced	2
2	lrg. green onions, chopped	2
1	cup slightly-thawed green peas	250 mL
1	cup shredded lettuce	250 mL
2	Tbs. dark soy sauce	25 mL
½	tsp. salt (or to taste)	2 mL

Garnish:
Diced tomato and green pepper

Fried rice provides a tasty way of converting leftovers into a one-dish meal or a complementary side dish. The embellishments are optional and flexible depending on what you have tucked away in the refrigerator. Day-old cooked rice (the long-grain variety) works best.

1. Separate grains of rice with hands. Set aside.
2. In wok or heavy skillet, cook beaten eggs in 1Tbs./15 mL hot oil (like a thin omelette). Set aside and shred into fine strips.
3. Heat remaining 2 Tbs./25 mL oil in pan over medium-high heat and stir-fry meat, celery, and green onions for 2-3 minutes. Add rice, stirring constantly until heated through.
4. Mix in green peas and lettuce, then the soy sauce and salt (both to taste). Will stand for a short while over low heat, but cover and stir occasionally.
5. Transfer to serving bowl and garnish with shredded egg, diced tomato and green pepper. Serve immediately.

* Use barbecued pork, cooked chicken or ham. Tiny shrimps are nice, but should not be added at this point. Mix them in towards end of cooking so that they will retain their pink colour and fresh taste. Should you not wish to use meat, simply add more vegetables.

RICE PILAV with CURRANTS and PINE NUTS

Simmer: 20-25 min.
Serves: 4-6

Rice with a Middle-Eastern flavour. Excellent with roast lamb or shish-a-bobs.

3	Tbs. butter or margarine	50 mL
1	med. onion, finely chopped	1
1½	cups raw long grain rice	375 mL
2	cups good chicken broth	500 mL
1	tsp. dried dillweed	5 mL
½	tsp. salt	2 mL
¼	tsp. pepper	1 mL
Extras:		
⅓	cup pine nuts, browned	75 mL
⅓	cup dried currants	75 mL

1. In heavy, medium-size saucepan, melt butter. Add onion and saute until tender. Add rice and stir to coat.
2. Next add broth, dillweed, salt and pepper. Bring to a boil and when most of the liquid has evaporated, reduce the heat to low. Cover tightly and let simmer, undisturbed for 20-25 minutes.
3. Meanwhile, saute pine nuts in a little oil until golden. Drain and add to rice along with currants. Fluff lightly with fork. Cover. Will keep hot, off heat for a short while.

WILD RICE with MUSHROOMS

Oven: 350F/180C
Bake: 1 hr.
Serves: 4

1	cup wild rice	250 mL
2	Tbs. butter or margarine	25 mL
1	sm. onion, finely minced	1
2	cups good chicken broth	500 mL
½	tsp. salt (or to taste)	2 mL
	Extras:	
2	Tbs. butter or margarine	25 mL
½	lb. fresh mushrooms, sliced	250 g
2	Tbs. minced parsley	25 mL
¼	cup chopped pecans	50 mL

1. Preheat oven. Rinse wild rice in several changes of water. Drain well. In a heavy medium-size saucepan, melt the butter and saute onion until tender.
2. Add rice, stirring well to coat. Pour in broth and salt to taste. Let come to a boil and then transfer directly to lightly-greased casserole. Cover tightly with foil. Bake in preheated oven for 1 hour or until tender and liquid is absorbed.
3. Shortly before rice is done, melt the extra butter in a medium skillet. Add mushrooms and parsley, cooking 5 minutes. If there is excess liquid, stir and cook until most of it has evaporated.
4. Add pecans. Top rice with this mixture. Will keep for a short while in warm oven. Mix lightly with fork before serving.

Wild rice is not really rice at all, but rather the kernel of an aquatic grass indigenous to the shallow lakes and waterways of Minnesota, Wisconsin, Manitoba, and Ontario. Much of it is still harvested in the traditional Indian manner — by hand in a canoe or skiff. Wild rice with its wonderful chewy texture and nutty flavour makes a natural complement to wild meat and fowl.

HERBED LEMON ORZO

Serves: 4

The tiny rice-shaped pasta called "Orzo" beautifully complements any kind of fish, meat, or poultry dish. Use it in place of rice or barley; also great in soups. A cinch to prepare.

1½	cups uncooked orzo	375 mL
	Boiling water — Salt	
4	Tbs. butter (or half olive oil)	60 mL
½	med. onion, finely chopped	½
1	med. clove garlic, minced	1
¼	cup minced parsley	50 mL
2	tsp. grated lemon rind	10 mL
¼	tsp. salt (or to taste)	1 mL
¼	tsp. freshly-ground pepper	1 mL
	Grated Parmesan cheese to top	

1. Cook orzo in a large pot of boiling water with salt added. When "al dente" (firm, but tender — will take 8-10 minutes), drain in colander and run under cold water to cool. Set aside.

2. Heat butter in a wide skillet. Add onion and garlic, and gently saute until golden. Stir in drained orzo, cooking over medium-low heat until warmed through. Add parsley, rind, salt and pepper (both to taste). Serve immediately with Parmesan.

BARLEY-MUSHROOM PILAF

Oven: 350F/180C
Bake: 1 hr.
Serves: 4-6

1	lrg. onion, chopped	1
4	Tbs. butter or margarine	60 mL
½	lb. fresh mushrooms, sliced	250 g
1	cup medium barley	250 mL
3	cups beef or chicken broth	750 mL

Salt and pepper, if required
Optional:
Minced parsley
Diced cooked bacon
Toasted pine nuts or almonds

Barley is a cereal grain more widely used in Europe than in North America. It's used in breads, soups, stews, and casseroles such as this one. Generally, the whiter and more "pearled" the barley, the less nutrients left in it. Most recipes call for the medium grain.

1. Preheat oven. In a large pot, saute chopped onions in melted butter until tender. Add mushrooms, cooking briefly, 2-3 minutes.
2. Stir in barley. Then add broth and seasonings, if necessary. Bring to a boil and then transfer to a greased casserole. Cover. Bake 1 hour or until barley is tender. May be made ahead up to this point.
3. If casserole is to be reheated, bring it to room temperature first. Serve piping hot. Top with parsley, diced bacon, or toasted nuts.

MACARONI and CHEESE

Oven: 350F/180C
Bake: 30 min
Serves: 4-6

2	cup elbow macaroni	500 mL
	Boiling water — Salt	
	Sauce:	
¼	cup butter or margarine	50 mL
2	Tbs. all-purpose flour	25 mL
1½	cups milk	375 mL
1½	cups grated cheddar	375 mL
1	tsp. salt (or to taste)	5 mL
¼	tsp. pepper	1 mL
¼	tsp. dry mustard	1 mL
	Topping:	
1	lrg. tomato, sliced	1
½	cup grated cheddar	125 mL

It's a cinch to measure grated cheese if you know that 4 oz./125 g of cheese equals 1 cup/250 mL grated. For this particular dish, use half medium-half mature or just mature to give it a nice, nippy flavour.

1. Cook macaroni in a large pot of boiling water with salt added. When al dente (slightly resistant to the bite), drain in colander.

2. In a large saucepan, melt butter. Stir in flour and cook, stirring for 3 minutes. Add milk and whisk or stir vigorously until smooth and well-blended. Mix in cheese, salt, pepper, and mustard, all to taste. Do not let boil.

3. Remove sauce from heat and add macaroni. Pour into greased 9 in./23 cm sq. pan or casserole. Top with sliced tomatoes and additional cheese. Bake in preheated oven until golden and completely heated through. Serve piping hot.

FETTUCCINE and GREEN CABBAGE

Serves: 4

Here's a refreshing contrast in textures and colours to complement just about any poultry or meat dish. Delicious, too. Use any kind of broad noodles from your favourite pasta shop.

2	cups shredded green cabbage	500 mL
1	tsp. salt	5 mL
3	Tbs. butter or margarine	50 mL
½	tsp. granulated sugar	2 mL
½	tsp. dried basil leaves	2 mL
¼	tsp. freshly ground pepper	1 mL
12	oz. fresh fettuccine	350 g
	Boiling water with salt added	

1. Place cabbage in colander and sprinkle with salt. Let stand about 30 minutes until wilted. Rinse under cold water and drain thoroughly.

2. In a wide skillet (wok works well here), melt butter and briefly saute cabbage. Sprinkle with sugar, basil, and pepper. Cook uncovered, stirring constantly until crisp-tender. Do not overcook — cabbage should remain green. Keep warm while pasta is cooking.

3. Cook pasta in a large pot of boiling salted water until "al dente" (just tender). Drain and immediately toss with cabbage. Adjust seasonings. Serve right away.

VARIATION: In place of cabbage, substitute unpeeled zucchini, cut into lengthwise shreds. Prepare in same manner as cabbage.

SPAETZLE with SPINACH and ONION

Serves: 4

8	oz. pkg. spaetzle	250	g
6	cups boiling water	1.5	L
4	Tbs. butter or margarine	60	mL
1	sm. onion, finely minced	1	
1	pkg. frozen chopped spinach	340	g
½	tsp. salt	2	mL
¼	tsp. pepper	1	mL

1. Completely thaw frozen spinach and squeeze to remove excess moisture. Cook spaetzle to "al dente" stage in a large pot of boiling water with salt added, about 15 minutes.
2. While spaetzle is cooking, melt the butter in a wide skillet. Add onion and briefly saute. Stir in chopped spinach and season with salt and pepper to taste. Keep warm.
3. Drain spaetzle and add to the hot spinach-onion mixture. May be kept for a short while in warm oven.

Spaetzle or Spatzen: a German term translated to mean "little sparrows". The tiny egg dumplings or noodles are an excellent accompaniment to most meat dishes, in particular stews. Ready-made spaetzle is available from delis and the specialty section of many supermarkets.

FARMHOUSE BREAKFAST

Serves: 4.

Leftover potatoes or potatoes cooked the night before are recommended for this hearty meal-in-one.

4	med. potatoes, cooked	4
6	slices bacon	6
1	tsp. cooking oil	5 mL
1	med. onion, chopped	1
6	lrg. eggs	6
½	tsp. salt	2 mL
¼	tsp. pepper	1 mL
	Chopped green onion	

1. Finely dice the cooked and cooled potatoes. Set aside. In wide skillet (preferably cast iron), cook bacon in a little oil until golden crisp. With slotted spatula, remove slices to drain on paper towelling.
2. To hot pan drippings, add onion and gently saute until tender. Next, add potatoes and brown them lightly. Add oil, if necessary.
3. Reduce heat. Beat eggs with salt and pepper. Pour over potato mixture, cooking until eggs are just barely set and top is still moist.
4. Sprinkle with diced or crumbled bacon and green onions. Cut into wedges. Bring to the table and serve straight from skillet.

GOLDEN-CRISP BACON: For bacon that looks picture-beautiful, coat each slice with all-purpose flour. Pat off excess and pan-fry in a wide skillet with a thin film of vegetable oil. Bacon will be golden and crisp...just the way it looks in the magazines. And shrinkage will be at a minimum.

OVERNIGHT BRUNCH

Oven: 350F/180C
Bake: 45-55 min.
Serves: 6-8

A tasty strata made the night before paves the way to a relaxed morning with family or friends. Serve with warm croissants or tiny brioche and a fresh fruit tray.

16	slices sandwich bread	16
8	thin slices ham	8
8	thin slices cheese	8
	Egg Mixture:	
6	lrg. eggs	6
3	cups milk	750 mL
1	tsp. Worcestershire sauce	5 mL
½	tsp. dry mustard	2 mL
½	tsp. salt	2 mL
2	sm. green onions, chopped	2
1	sm. green pepper, chopped	1
	Topping:	
½	cup butter, melted	125 mL
2	cups crushed potato chips	500 mL

1. Trim off crusts from bread and fit into well buttered 13x9 in./3.5 L pan. Cover with slices of ham and then cheese. Place remaining bread slices on top (like sandwiches).

2. In large mixing bowl, beat eggs. Mix in milk, Worcestershire, mustard, and salt. Stir in chopped green onions and green pepper. Pour over bread. Cover and refrigerate overnight.

3. Next morning, preheat oven. Drizzle top of casserole with melted butter. Sprinkle with crushed chips. Bake uncovered until bubbly and completely heated through. Let stand 10 minutes before serving.

SALMON KEDGEREE

Serves: 2-3

A simplified version of kedgeree, originally a Hindu dish adapted to British tastes. Served over rice, this lightly curried salmon presentation makes an excellent on-the-spur-of-the-moment dinner for two. Serve with salad of crisp greens and watercress.

1	med. tin red salmon	220 g
2	lrg. eggs, hard-cooked	2
	Sauce:	
3	Tbs. butter or margarine	50 mL
1	med. onion, chopped	1
1	Tbs. curry powder	15 mL
⅛	tsp. cayenne, for hotness	1 mL
¼	lb. fresh mushrooms, sliced	125 g
2	Tbs. all-purpose flour	25 mL
1	cup milk or broth	250 mL
1	tsp. fresh lemon juice	5 mL
½	tsp. salt (or to taste)	2 mL
¼	tsp. pepper	1 mL
	Minced parsley for garnish	

1. Drain salmon, reserving liquid. Slice cooked eggs and set aside.
2. In medium saucepan, melt butter. Add onion, stirring and cooking until tender and golden. Add spices and stir for 1-2 minutes.
3. Mix in mushrooms, sauteeing briefly. Sprinkle in flour and cook, stirring for 3 minutes.
4. Add milk and reserved salmon juices, whisking or stirring until mixture is well blended and thickened.
5. Add lemon juice and seasonings to taste. Sauce may be made ahead and kept warm or reheated.
6. Just before serving, gently stir in salmon and eggs, cooking only to heat through. Pour over hot cooked rice and sprinkle with a little parsley. Serve immediately.

TUNA STUFFED BUNWICHES

Oven: 350F/180C
Bake: 25 min.
Yields: 6

A great make-ahead for some easy, light eating. Heat up last minute.

6	Kaiser or hamburger buns	6
	Soft butter or margarine	
	Filling:	
1	tin solid tuna, drained	198 g
3	lrg. hard-cooked eggs, chopped	3
1	cup grated cheddar cheese	250 mL
1	sm. green pepper, diced	1
1	lrg. green onion, chopped	1
3	Tbs. chopped sweet pickle	50 mL
½	cup mayonnaise (to bind)	125 mL
½	tsp. salt (or to taste)	2 mL
¼	tsp. pepper	1 mL

1. Split and spread buns with butter or margarine.
2. In mixing bowl, break tuna into chunks and combine with remaining ingredients. Fill buns and wrap in foil. Refrigerate until serving time.
3. Preheat oven. Heat foil-wrapped buns until hot, about 25 minutes.

VARIATION: Try leftover roasted chicken or turkey meat, about 1 cup/250 mL. Leave out green pepper and sweet pickles, and substitute ¼ cup/50 mL chopped salted peanuts. May also be broiled open-faced for 2-3 minutes. Good!

TOAD-in-the-HOLE

Oven: 400F/200C
Bake: 30-40 min.
Serves: 4

A British tradition. Nowadays, most cooks use pork sausages, replacing the leftovers from Sunday's roast. Toad-in-the-Hole served with a crisp green salad makes a comforting meal for a brisk winter day.

1	lb. regular pork sausages	500 g
1	Tbs. cooking oil	15 mL
	Batter:	
2	lrg. eggs, room temperature	2
1	cup milk	250 mL
1	cup all-purpose flour	250 mL
½	tsp. salt	2 mL

1. Preheat oven. Lightly brown sausages in hot oil. Transfer sausages plus 3 Tbs./50 mL drippings to a cast iron skillet or a small roasting pan. Place in hot oven.

2. Meanwhile prepare batter. In a large mixing bowl, beat together eggs and milk. Add flour and salt, mixing just until smooth and well-blended. If using a mixer, beat at low speed for 1-2 minutes. Do not overbeat, otherwise batter will not rise to its maximum height.

3. Pour batter over hot sausages and drippings. Bake until puffed and golden, about 30 minutes. Do not open oven door during baking as batter may collapse. Serve immediately.

TOURTIERE

Oven: 425F/220C
Bake: 35-40 min.
Serves: 4-6

Tourtiere is the traditional spiced pork pie served in many French-Canadian homes early Christmas morning after Midnight Mass. It is delicious served with chili sauce or a homemade chutney.

Pastry for 2-crust pie
Filling:

1	med. potato, peeled	1	
1	lb. lean ground pork	500	g
1	med. onion, minced	1	
1	med. clove garlic, crushed	1	
½	tsp. crumbled thyme	2	mL
½	tsp. savory or sage	2	mL
½	tsp. salt	2	mL
¼	tsp. ground cloves	1	mL
¼	tsp. dry mustard	1	mL

1. Use your favourite pastry recipe or the one for Cornish Pasties. It's excellent for this!
2. To make filling: first boil the potato until tender. Reserve ½ cup/125 mL cooking liquid. Mash potato and set aside.
3. Next, combine remaining ingredients in a wide, heavy saucepan with reserved potato water. Bring to a boil and then reduce heat to medium-low. Cook, uncovered for about 20 minutes.
4. When most of the liquid has dissipated, remove from heat. Discard garlic and mix in mashed potato. Cool.
5. Preheat oven. Roll out pastry to fit 9 in./23 cm pie plate. Turn pork mixture into shell. Moisten edges and cover with top crust. Trim and then crimp edges to seal. Prick top. May be made ahead and frozen.
6. Bake 35-40 minutes until golden. Serve warm.

CORNISH PASTIES

Makes: 4 lrg.

Cornish pasties were the traditional lunch of the Cornish tin miners in England. The meat and vegetable-filled turnovers were pointed at both ends, designed to be carried in the pocket. Pasties make excellent picnic fare.

Pastry:
2	cups all-purpose flour	500 mL
½	tsp. baking powder	2 mL
½	tsp. salt	2 mL
1	cup lard or shortening	250 mL
½	cup cold water	125 mL
	Extra flour for rolling	

Filling:
½	lb. boneless round steak	250 g
1	med. onion, chopped	1
1	med. potato, diced	1
1	med. carrot, diced	1
1	cup diced yellow turnip	250 mL
¼	cup light broth or water	50 mL
½	tsp. salt	2 mL
¼	tsp. pepper	1 mL

Glaze:
1	sm. egg, well beaten	1

1. In a large mixing bowl, combine flour, baking powder, and salt. Add lard and cut in, using pastry blender or two knives. Mixture should resemble coarse crumbs. Sprinkle in just enough water to lightly bind particles together. Form ball without overmixing — otherwise crust will be tough. Chill briefly.

2. Meanwhile prepare filling. Cut steak into very small cubes. Place in a mixing bowl along with diced vegetables, broth, and seasonings.

3. Divide dough into 4 balls. On well-floured surface, roll out into 7 in./18 cm circles. Place one-quarter of the filling onto centre of each.

4. Brush edges with beaten egg. Bring sides of pastry up to middle and roll under to form double band. Flute, crimp, or simply press together. Brush with glaze. May be made ahead up to this point, but keep chilled.

5. Preheat oven to 450F/230C. Bake pasties on ungreased baking sheet for 10 minutes. Then reduce temperature to 325F/160C and bake for an additional 1 hour until golden. Cool pasties on rack.

NOTE: If you wish, use your own pastry recipe or a commercial brand; but make enough for a 2-crust pie.

GOLDEN-FRIED MOZZARELLA

Serves: 2

8	oz. Mozzarella cheese*	250 g
2	Tbs. all-purpose flour	25 mL
1	lrg. egg, well beaten	1
½	cup fine bread crumbs	125 mL
¼	cup olive oil	50 mL
2	Tbs. butter	25 mL

For an exciting presentation, serve over herb-flavoured tomato sauce (your own is best here). Also very good as is, with French bread and a tossed green salad.

1. Slice Mozzarella about ¼ in./0.5 cm thick. Dust pieces all over with flour. Then dip into beaten egg, coating thoroughly with crumbs.

2. Heat oil and butter together in a wide skillet over medium heat. Add cheese, a few slices at a time, frying just until bottom is golden. Turn only once and brown quickly on the other side. Do not overcook, otherwise cheese will ooze out.

3. Remove with wide, slotted spatula. Drain and serve immediately. Excellent with the following tomato sauce.

* Other cheeses to try: Provolone, wedges of Camembert, chevre (fresh goat cheese).

SPRIGHTLY TOMATO SAUCE: In a stainless saucepan, heat 3 Tbs./50 mL olive oil until rippling hot. Add the following ingredients, all finely chopped: 1 medium carrot, 1 medium rib celery, 1 small onion, and 1 large clove garlic. Cook, stirring for about 15 minutes until tender. Add 1 — 398 mL tin Italian plum tomatoes (without draining) and simmer covered, 30 minutes. Add 1 Tbs./15 mL chopped fresh basil leaves or 1 tsp./5 mL dried with ½ tsp./2 mL salt and ¼ tsp./1 mL pepper both to taste. May be reheated. Also good over fresh pasta or tortellini. Makes: 2 cups/500 mL.

PIZZA in a JIFFY

Oven: 400F/200C
Bake: 20 min.
Serves: 4-6

Start with one of those crusty Italian loaves from the supermarket bakery. Add a batch of pre-made tomato sauce from your kitchen. Then jazz up the whole thing with whatever happens to strike your fancy...and you've got a winner.

1	lrg. loaf Italian bread	1
1	lb. good Mozzarella cheese	500 g
	Sauce:	
2	Tbs. good olive oil	25 mL
1	med. onion, finely chopped	1
1	lrg. clove garlic, minced	1
1	sm. tin tomato sauce	213 mL
1	sm. tin tomato paste	156 mL
2	tsp. granulated sugar	10 mL
1	tsp. dried leaf oregano	5 mL
1	tsp. dried basil leaves	5 mL
½	tsp. salt	2 mL
½	tsp. coarse ground pepper	2 mL

Toppings:
Salami, green pepper, shrimp
Fresh thinly sliced mushrooms
Cooked pork sausages, olives

1. Split bread in half lengthwise. Keep wrapped. Shred cheese on coarse grater. Wrap and set aside.
2. Make sauce ahead. Heat oil in heavy saucepan and gently saute onion and garlic. Stir in remaining sauce ingredients. Simmer 20-25 min. Cool. May be stored in glass jar.
3. Preheat oven to 400F/200C. Spread sauce over cut sides of loaf. Cover evenly with grated cheese and then top with desired toppings.
4. Place on large baking sheet and bake for about 20 minutes or until bubbly and heated through. Let stand briefly before cutting.

PASTA with HERBED CLAM SAUCE

Serves: 2

The Italian term, "al dente" describes pasta that has been cooked just to the point that it is still firm and chewy. It should never be raw or hard at the core. Nor should it have a floury taste or be cooked to the mushy stage.

12	oz. fresh linguine	350 g
4	qts. boiling water — salt	4 L
	Sauce:	
1	tin whole baby clams	142 g
4	Tbs. butter or margarine	60 mL
2	Tbs. good olive oil	25 mL
1	med. onion, chopped	1
1	lrg. clove garlic, minced	1
¼	cup minced parsley	50 mL
1	Tbs. minced fresh basil	15 mL
¼	tsp. salt (or to taste)	1 mL
¼	tsp. freshly-ground pepper	1 mL
	Freshly-grated Parmesan	

1. Cook pasta in a large pot with boiling water and 1 Tbs./15 mL salt added for about 3 minutes or until "al dente". Drain in colander and briefly run under cold water.

2. Drain clams, reserving liquor (about ½ cup/125 mL; otherwise add dry white wine to make up that amount). In large wide skillet (enough to accommodate pasta), heat butter and olive oil together. Add onion and garlic, gently cooking until tender.

3. Add liquor from clams, the parsley, basil, salt and lots of pepper, both to taste. Simmer briefly. Add clams just to heat through. Do not overcook; otherwise clams will toughen.

4. Add pasta and toss lightly with two forks. When heated through, lift onto warm platter(s) and serve immediately with Parmesan on the side.

OCEAN GARDEN PASTA

Serves: 4

¾	lb. fettuccine	350 g
	Boiling water — salt	
¾	lb. fresh scallops	350 g
3	Tbs. butter or margarine	50 mL
½	cup dry white wine	125 mL
1½	cups sliced fresh mushrooms	375 mL
¾	cup sliced green onions	175 mL
1½	cups heavy cream	375 mL
1½	tsp. dried dillweed	7 mL
½	tsp. salt	2 mL
¼	tsp. freshly ground pepper	1 mL

For pasta lovers. From Vancouver cooking instructor, Kasey Wilson. When her book, "The Granville Island Cookbook" was being promoted, this recipe made a great hit. Fresh pasta makes all the difference here.

1. Cook fettuccine in 4 qts./4 L boiling water with 2 Tbs./25 mL salt added. Fresh pasta will take only 2-3 minutes, and dry pasta about 8 minutes to reach the al dente (firm, but tender) stage. Drain in colander, running under cold water. Set aside.

2. Slice scallops in half horizontally. Melt butter in wide skillet and add wine. Stir in scallops, mushrooms, and green onions. Cook 3-4 minutes, stirring occasionally until scallops turn translucent. Do not overcook; otherwise they will toughen. With slotted spoon, remove scallop mixture to plate and keep warm.

3. Add cream to the same skillet and reduce until cream starts to lightly coat a spoon, about 10 minutes. Remove from heat. Add dillweed, salt and pepper, and the scallop mixture. Add fettuccine and heat through. Serve immediately.

LIBERAL LASAGNE

Oven: 350F/180C
Bake: 50 min.
Serves: 8-10

Lasagne never goes out of style around our place. My favourite version comes from the files of friend, Joy Bradbury. "Musts" to accompany this include a crisp green salad and lots of garlic bread.

Sauce:

4	Tbs. olive or salad oil	60 mL
1	lrg. onion, finely chopped	1
1	lrg. clove garlic, minced	1
2	Tbs. minced parsley	25 mL
1	lb. lean ground beef	500 g
2	tins Italian plum tomatoes	EA. 398 mL
2	tins undrained mushroom slices	EA. 284 mL
2	tins tomato paste	EA. 156 mL
2	Tbs. granulated sugar	25 mL
3	tsp. salt (or to taste)	15 mL
2	tsp. dried oregano leaves	10 mL
1	tsp. dried basil leaves	5 mL
½	tsp. freshly-ground pepper	2 mL

Extras:

½	pkg. lasagne noodles (10)	½
	Boiling water-Salt	
½	cup grated Parmesan cheese	125 mL
1	lb. ricotta or cottage cheese	500 g
1	lb. mozzarella cheese, grated	500 g
	Minced parsley	

1. Sauce: Heat oil in a large pot. Add onion, garlic, and parsley, sauteing until tender. Add beef and brown; drain off excess oil.

2. Add remaining ingredients. Bring to a boil reduce heat and cook uncovered for about 2 hours or until sauce is very thick and slightly reduced in volume. May be made ahead and stored in refrigerator.

3. Cook lasagne noodles in large pot of boiling water with salt added, for about 15 minutes or until "al dente" (tender, but firm to the bite). Drain and rinse briefly under cold water.

4. Cover bottom of greased 13x9 in./4 L lasagne pan with thin film of sauce. Put on HALF portions of the following in order given: noodles, sauce, Parmesan, ricotta, and mozzarella. Repeat ending with mozzarella.

5. Preheat oven. Cover lasagne with foil. Bake about 50 minutes, removing foil during last half hour of baking.

6. Sprinkle with parsley. Let "set" for at least 10 minutes before serving. Cut into large squares and serve while still piping hot.

CACCIATORE on the SLOPES

Serves: 4

4	med. chicken breasts (single)	4
⅓	cup flour (for coating)	75 mL
¾	tsp. salt	5 mL
½	tsp. pepper	2 mL
2	Tbs. vegetable oil	25 mL
	Sauce:	
½	lb. fresh mushrooms, sliced	250 g
1	sm. green pepper, diced	1
1	sm. onion, chopped	1
½	cup broth or dry white wine	125 mL
1	jar good spaghetti sauce	398 mL
2	Tbs. minced parsley or basil	25 mL

1. Coat chicken breasts with mixture of flour, salt, and pepper. Brown in hot oil. Remove to platter and set aside.
2. To same skillet, add mushrooms, green pepper, and onion. Saute gently until tender.
3. Add broth or wine. Return chicken and accumulated juices to pan. Let come to a boil. Reduce heat. Cover and simmer for 30 minutes.
4. Add sauce. At this point, dish may be made ahead. Just before serving time, bring the whole thing to a low simmer and heat through. Sprinkle with lots of freshly chopped parsley or basil.

The term "Cacciatore" is applied to poultry or meat that has been prepared with tomatoes, onions, wine, garlic, and herbs. This recipe is made easy with commercially prepared spaghetti sauce, a number of which are excellent. Serve over pasta or rice accompanied with a crisp green salad.

CARIBBEAN CURRIED CHICKEN

Serves: 4

An island favourite from my friend, Marcia. Delicious served with rice pilau or plain steamed rice. Garam masala is an aromatic mixture of spices frequently used in Indian cookery.

3	lb. fryer chicken, segmented	1.5 kg
1/3	cup butter or margarine	75 mL
2	med. onions, finely chopped	2
2	lrg. cloves garlic, minced	2
2	Tbs. minced root ginger	25 mL
2	tsp. garam masala (spice)	10 mL
2	tsp. good curry powder	10 mL
8	cardamom seeds, crushed	8
1/2	tsp. salt (or to taste)	2 mL
1/4	tsp. crushed dried chiles (6)	1 mL
1/4	cup water or chicken broth	50 mL

1. Skin chicken pieces and set aside.
2. In a large heavy skillet, melt butter and gently saute onions for about 10 minutes until golden. Add garlic and ginger. Cook another 5 minutes.
3. Add remaining spices and seasonings, all according to your tastes. Stir and cook briefly. Mix in chicken and cook until opaque. Then add water or broth.
4. Let mixture come to a boil. Reduce heat. Cover and let simmer on low setting for about 45 minutes or until chicken is tender. Check occasionally, adding extra liquid if necessary.
5. This dish is best made ahead and reheated.

CREOLE JAMBALAYA

Simmer: 35 min.
Serves: 4

Creole cookery is a colourful blend of French, Spanish, and African cuisines enriched by the Indian gift of New World delicacies native to the state of Louisiana. Jambalaya is a savory combination of rice, meats, sometimes seafood, and spices.

6	med. chicken thighs	6
	Salt and pepper	
2	Tbs. cooking oil	25 mL
1	med. onion, chopped	1
1	lrg. clove garlic, minced	1
1	med. green pepper, chopped	1
2	Tbs. minced parsley	25 mL
2	cups cubed leftover ham*	500 mL
1½	cups raw long-grain rice	375 mL
1	med. bay leaf, crumbled	1
½	tsp. dried thyme leaves	2 mL
½	tsp. chili powder	2 mL
½	tsp. salt	2 mL
½	tsp. freshly ground pepper	2 mL
⅛	tsp. cayenne (for hotness)	1 mL
3	cups good beef broth	750 mL
	Minced parsley for garnish	

1. Pat chicken dry. Sprinkle with salt and pepper. Heat oil in heavy skillet. Add chicken and brown. Remove to platter.
2. To same pan, add onion, garlic, green pepper, and parsley. Saute slowly until tender, about 8 minutes.
3. Add cubed ham, cooking and stirring 5 minutes. Stir in rice, all herbs, and the seasonings, mixing well.
4. Pour in broth and let come to a boil. Lay chicken pieces on top. Cover tightly and reduce heat to very low simmer. Cook 20 minutes without disturbing.

5. Gently stir mixture. Simmer covered for an additional 15 minutes, stirring occasionally. Taste for seasonings. Garnish with parsley. Serve piping hot.

* Use smoked Bavarian-type sausage or leftover cooked pork sausages (about 6), sliced into chunks.

POOR MAN'S OMELETTE

**Cook: 20 min.
Serves: 4**

This omelette is laden with crusty-golden potatoes and lots of greenery. Serve with salsa, store-bought or homemade (recipe in appetizer section). A good meal stretcher. Leftovers make marvellous sandwiches.

1. Finely cube 2 large, well-scrubbed potatoes, without peeling. In a medium skillet (cast iron is excellent), heat ¼ cup/50 mL olive oil until rippling hot. Add potatoes and cook until golden and tender, about 10 minutes.
2. Stir in the following ingredients, all chopped: ½ bunch green onions, a handful of parsley sprigs, and 2 cloves garlic. Cook briefly and then reduce heat. Pat potato mixture evenly over bottom of pan.
3. Lightly beat together: 6 large eggs, ¼ cup/50 mL water, ½ tsp./2 mL salt, and ¼ tsp./1 mL freshly-ground pepper. Pour over potatoes. Cover and cook slowly until bottom is crusty and top is set, but still moist.
4. Loosen edges and bottom of omelette. Place a platter over can and onto it, carefully invert the omelette. May also be served straight from skillet. Cut into wedges. Good served hot or cold.

CHIMICHANGAS

Oven: 350F/180C
Bake: 15-20 min.
Serves: 4

These Mexican filled tortillas make a substantial meal-in-one. And they are so much fun to assemble. The meat-bean mixture may be made ahead. To prevent the tortillas from going soggy, do not stuff them too far ahead of time.

1	lb. lean ground beef	500 g
1	Tbs. cooking oil	15 mL
1	med. onion, chopped	1
1	lrg. clove garlic, minced	1
1	lrg. tomato, seeded, chopped	1
1	cup refried beans	250 mL
½	cup Mexican red sauce*	125 mL
1	Tbs. chili powder	15 mL
1	tsp. dried leaf oregano	5 mL
½	tsp. ground cumin seed	2 mL
½	tsp. salt (or to taste)	2 mL
8	lrg. wheat flour tortillas	8
	Vegetable oil for cooking	
	Toppings:	
	Grated cheddar or Monterey Jack	
	Shredded lettuce	
	Chopped green onions	
	Dairy sour cream	

1. Brown beef in a little hot oil. Add onion and garlic, cooking until tender. Stir in tomato, beans, sauce, spices, and seasonings to taste. Keep warm.

2. Quickly fry tortillas, one at a time in just a little hot oil until golden on both sides, 1-2 minutes. Do not let crispen. Drain on paper towelling and immediately spoon 3 Tbs./50 mL warm filling down the centre.

3. Roll up and place seam-side down in a 13x9 in./3 L baking pan. Bake in preheated oven, uncovered for 15-20 minutes or until heated through. Do not overbake.

4. While chimichangas are baking, attractively mound garnishings on a large serving platter. Serve 2 chimichangas per person. Let each guest help himself to desired toppings.

* You may use Taco, Enchilada, or Salsa sauce here.

REFRIED BEANS
(Frijoles Refritos)

Makes: 2½ cups/ 625 mL

The term "refried" should not be taken literally to mean "fried again". It can also refer to "very" or "thoroughly". In this case, the beans are given only one thorough frying, and that's it! The secret for good refried beans is in the fat. Most Mexican cooks use home-rendered lard, but any well-flavoured fat such as bacon drippings will do.

1. Sort out 1 cup/250 mL dried pinto or pink beans to remove foreign particles. Place beans in a large saucepan with hot water to cover. Let stand overnight.

2. Drain and rinse beans. Again, cover them with boiling water. Bring to a boil. Add 1 small onion, chopped; cook partially covered over gentle heat until beans are very tender and easy to mash, about 3 hours.

3. Drain off liquid and mash beans with a potato masher, adding about 4 Tbs./60 mL very hot lard or bacon drippings. Cook, stirring often until beans are thickened and fat is well absorbed. Beans may be partially or completely mashed. Salt to taste. May be reheated.

BURRITOS

Serves: 4-6

If you like tacos, you'll love burritos. Ready-made flour tortillas from the supermarket eliminate the most time-consuming step. Since burritos are meant to be eaten out of hand, they make a perfect meal for the outdoors.

Filling:

2	lb. coarse ground meat*	1 kg
3	Tbs. cooking oil	50 mL
1	lrg. onion, chopped	1
2	lrg. cloves garlic, minced	2
2	tsp. chili powder	10 mL
1½	tsp. ground cumin seed	7 mL
1	tsp. dried leaf oregano	5 mL
1	tsp. salt (or to taste)	5 mL
¼	tsp. cayenne	1 mL
½	cup bottled taco sauce	125 mL
⅓	cup water	75 mL

Condiments:
Shredded lettuce; Grated cheddar or jack cheese; Diced tomato, green pepper, cucumber, or green onion; Sliced avocado; Salsa or taco sauce; Dairy sour cream, Refried beans

Wrappers:

1	pkg. lrg. flour tortillas (10)	1

1. In wide skillet over medium heat, brown meat in hot oil. Add onion and garlic, cooking until tender. Drain off excess fat. Season with spices according to your own tastes. Add taco sauce and water.

2. Cover and let mixture simmer gently for 30 minutes or until meat is tender. Mixture should be on the thick, but moist side. May be made ahead and reheated with a little water to prevent drying out.

3. Arrange whatever condiments you wish in separate rows on shallow serving platter or tray. Wrap and keep chilled until serving time.

4. Shortly before serving time, warm tortillas as directed on package or cook them one by one (both sides) over medium-high heat in an ungreased electric skillet just until brown blisters begin to form. The breads should remain soft and supple.

5. Wrap cooked tortillas in tea towel and slide into plastic bag to steam and keep warm. Each person then stuffs his own tortilla with meat and condiments.

* Buy boneless chuck steak or a lean pork roast. Cube and then grind it coarsely (a food processor is excellent for this).

GRINGO CHILI

Simmer: 1 hr.
Serves: 4

In true Tex-Mex fashion, this one calls for cubed or coarse-ground meat, lots of garlic, cumin, oregano, and a good dose of red chiles for added fire. Pinto beans are served on the side. Guaranteed to melt down your esophagus.

1½	lbs. lean chuck steak	750 mL
3	Tbs. cooking oil	50 mL
2	med. onions, chopped	2
2	lrg. cloves garlic, minced	2
2	Tbs. chili powder	25 mL
1	tsp. dried pequin chiles	5 mL
1	tsp. ground cumin seed	5 mL
1	tsp. paprika	5 mL
½	tsp. ground oregano	2 mL
½	tsp. granulated sugar	2 mL
2	cups light beef broth	500 mL
2	Tbs. tomato paste	25 mL
½	tsp. salt (or to taste)	2 mL
½	tsp. cracked black pepper	2 mL

1. Cut beef into ½ in./1.5 cm bits or grind it coarsely in your processor. Heat oil in large heavy pot (cast iron is excellent) and brown the meat. Add onions and garlic, cooking until most of the liquid has disappeared.

2. Add spices and sugar. Stir 2-3 minutes. Add broth, tomato paste, salt and pepper to taste. Bring to a boil. Reduce heat. Cover and simmer gently for about 1 hour, stirring from time to time. Sauce should be thickened and meat tender. May be reheated.

ENTREES

DEEP COVE FISH PATTIES

Saute: 3-5 min.
Serves: 4-6

Delicious with leftover fish such as salmon or cod. Fresh crabmeat, minced oysters, and well-drained clams (or a mixture) are good, too. Accompany with green mayonnaise.

2	cups cooked fish or seafood	500 g
1	lrg. egg, lightly beaten	1
½	cup dry bread crumbs	125 mL
¼	cup mayonnaise	50 mL
¼	cup heavy cream	50 mL
2	med. green onions, minced	2
2	Tbs. minced parsley	25 mL
½	tsp. dry mustard	2 mL
½	tsp. salt	2 mL
¼	tsp. pepper	1 mL
	Fine crumbs for coating	
	Butter or oil for sauteing	

1. Flake fish or seafood in a medium mixing bowl. Add remaining ingredients with salt and pepper to taste. Chill mixture for at least 2 hours to firm.
2. Form small patties or cakes and coat well in fine crumbs. Saute in hot butter for 3-5 minutes until golden-brown and heated through. May be served hot or cold.

EMERGENCY FISH CAKES: Drain 1 med. tin/220 g salmon, reserving juices. Flake and add remaining ingredients, replacing cream with salmon juices. Plain mashed potatoes may be used instead of bread crumbs.

WEI'S SALMON BARBECUE SAUCE

Yields: 1 cup/250 mL

2/3	cup Miracle Whip salad dressing	150 mL
1/3	cup butter or margarine, melted	75 mL
1	Tbs. regular white vinegar	15 mL
1	Tbs. (heaped) liquid honey	15 mL
½	tsp. dried dillweed	2 mL
	Squeeze fresh lemon juice	
	Salt and pepper (to taste)	

1. Combine the above ingredients until smooth and well blended. Brush sauce on both sides of salmon.
2. Grill approximately 6 in./15 cm from hot coals until browned. Turn; brush with more sauce and cook until top is glazed over and fish flakes easily with fork.
3. Serve extra sauce, warmed on the side.

This recipe won Vancouver resident, David Wei first place in a contest of Best BBQ Sauces sponsored by Western Living Magazine a few years back. Delicious with salmon fillets or steaks.

SALMON TERIYAKI

Serves: 4-6

A Japanese specialty marinated in a sweet shoyu (soya) mixture and then barbequed. Delicious! Use salmon steaks or fillets (with skin left on), measuring at least ¾ in./2 cm thick. Serve with rice and lightly sauteed vegetables.

6	med. pieces thick salmon	6
	Sauce:	
½	cup Japanese soy sauce	125 mL
¼	cup sake (rice wine)*	50 mL
2	Tbs. mirin (Japanese seasoning)	25 mL
2	Tbs. granulated sugar	25 mL
1	Tbs. vegetable oil	15 mL
1	med. clove garlic, minced	1
½	tsp. powdered ginger	2 mL
½	tsp. salt	2 mL

1. Pat fish dry with towelling and place in single layer in shallow glass dish.
2. In a small saucepan, combine the remaining sauce ingredients and heat briefly just to blend (do not boil). Pour over fish and let stand 1 hour at room temperature or 2-3 hours in refrigerator. Turn occasionally.
3. Just before cooking, adjust barbeque grill to highest rack; in oven, about 6 in./15 cm from broiler. Grease racks.
4. Cook salmon 10 minutes per inch/2.5 cm thickness of fish or just until fish flakes when prodded with fork. Do not overcook. Brush frequently with marinade. Serve with warm, leftover sauce.

* You may substitute sherry for the sake.

SCALLOPED OYSTERS

Oven: 350F/180C
Bake: 40 min.
Serves: 4-6

The little coppery Olympia oysters which are native to the Pacific Northwest are some of the finest to be found anywhere. Contrary to popular belief, oysters are not toxic in the months without the letter "r". The oyster is of less commercial value during its reproductive period as the flesh tends to turn soft and watery.

1	pt. fresh shucked oysters	½ L
2	cups coarsely crushed crackers	500 mL
2	sm. green onions, minced (opt.)	2
½	cup butter or margarine, melted	125 mL
	Cream:	
¾	cup cream, light or heavy	175 mL
¼	cup liquor from oysters	50 mL
1	tsp. Worcestershire sauce	5 mL
½	tsp. salt (or to taste)	2 mL
¼	tsp. cayenne	1 mL

1. Preheat oven. Drain oysters, reserving liquor. Combine crumbs and onions with melted butter. Spread ⅓ crumbs in lightly-greased 1½ qt./1.5 L baking dish or casserole.

2. Cover with half of the drained oysters (cut up, if large) and another ⅓ of the crumbs. Cover with remaining oysters.

3. Combine cream, oyster liquor, and seasonings to taste. Pour over oysters. Top with remaining crumbs. Bake uncovered in preheated oven for about 40 minutes or until nicely browned.

HOT SEAFOOD SALAD

Serves: 4-6

At Snappers Restaurant in False Creek, this dish rates as one of the top favourites. Chef Daniel Martinez takes the credit for this exciting presentation.

2	lrg. bunches young spinach	2
2	med. tomatoes, diced, seeded	2
½	cup sliced fresh mushrooms	125 mL
8	oz. fresh crabmeat	250 g
1	Tbs. butter	15 mL
1	Tbs. vegetable oil	15 mL
8	oz. fresh salmon, thick slices	250 g
8	oz. prawns, shelled, deveined	250 g
8	oz. baby scallops, drained	250 g
1	med. lemon, for juice	1
	Salt and pepper to taste	
	Dijon dressing (below)	
	Minced parsley & lemon wedges	

1. Wash and dry spinach, nipping off any coarse stems. Large leaves should be torn. Chill. Prepare dressing below.

2. Just before serving time, place spinach, diced tomatoes, mushrooms, and crab in a large bowl. Set aside.

3. In a wide skillet, heat butter and oil together. Add and briefly saute salmon slices, whole prawns, and last of all the bay scallops. Do not overcook.

4. Quickly toss the salad with dressing and arrange on individual platters. Top each serving with hot seafood. Garnish with minced parsley and lemon wedges. Serve immediately.

DRESSING: In blender or mixing bowl, combine ¼ cup/50 mL red wine vinegar, 1 Tbs./15 mL Dijon mustard, ½ tsp./2 mL salt, and ¼ tsp./1 mL freshly-ground pepper (both to taste). Add ¾ cup/175 mL salad oil in a thin stream, whirling or whisking until thickened. Let stand 15 minutes.

PAN-FRIED TROUT

Pan-fry: 8-10 min.
Serves: 4

4	med. fresh trout, cleaned	4
4	Tbs. all-purpose flour	60 mL
4	Tbs. yellow cornmeal	60 mL
½	tsp. salt	2 mL
¼	tsp. pepper	1 mL
4	Tbs. vegetable oil	60 mL
2	Tbs. butter or margarine	25 mL

One of the best ways of enjoying trout is also one of the simplest. The quick pan-frying method instantaneously seals in the juices and allows us to enjoy its sweet, delicate flavour.

1. Rinse off trout, leaving heads and tails in tact. Pat lightly with paper towelling.
2. On large piece of waxed paper, combine flour, cornmeal, salt, and pepper. Roll trout into mixture, coating both sides well.
3. Using a large wide skillet or electric frying pan over medium-high heat, swirl oil and butter together until hot.
4. Add trout, cooking uncovered, 4-5 minutes per side. Turn only once. Outside should be crisp-golden and the inside cooked and moist. Do not overcook. Serve immediately.

TO DE-BONE COOKED TROUT:
1. With dinner knife, separate top half of trout from bottom by running knife beneath backbone (right from head to tail). Bottom will be filleted portion.
2. With knife under spine and fork steadying top half, gently flip top half over.
3. Catch tail end of spine in tines of fork and lift it up, loosening spinal column with knife to remove skeleton and head in one piece.

SHRIMP in LEMON-GARLIC BUTTER

Saute: 3-5 min.
Serves: 2

Look for the large fresh shrimp in the shell, sometimes called "prawns" or "jumbos". Simply serve with fresh French bread to sop up the garlic butter.

1	lb. large raw shrimp	500 g
¼	cup butter	50 mL
¼	cup olive oil	50 mL
1	lrg. shallot, minced	1
1	med. clove garlic, minced	1
1	Tbs. fresh lemon juice	15 mL
½	tsp. salt (or to taste)	2 mL
2	Tbs. minced parsley	25 mL

Shell, devein, and wash shrimp, leaving tails in tact. Pat dry. Heat butter and oil in a medium skillet until sizzling hot. Add shallot, garlic, lemon juice, and salt. Swirl around for a second or two. Add shrimp and saute 3-5 minutes just until they turn a beautiful coral colour. Sprinkle with parsley and serve immediately.

F.O.B. SALMON with TOMATO STUFFING

Oven: 450F/230C
Bake: 45-55 min.
Serves: 6-8

A fabulous treatment for "fresh-off-the-boat" salmon, with red spring being our favourite. Accompany with a rice or potato dish.

5	lb. (approx.) fresh salmon	2 kg
	Salt and pepper	
	Thinly sliced lemon	
	Thinly sliced onion	
	Dillweed — Soft butter	
	Stuffing:	
1	med. onion, chopped	1
2	Tbs. butter or margarine	25 mL
2	cups finely cubed bread	500 mL
2	lrg. tomatoes, chopped, drained	2
2	Tbs. chopped fresh basil (opt.)	25 mL
½	tsp. salt	2 mL
¼	tsp. pepper	1 mL

1. Pat salmon (cavity, too) with towelling. Season lightly with salt and pepper. Place on large sheet of heavy duty foil with fish resting on HALF portions of sliced lemon and onion sprinkled with dillweed and soft butter bits.
2. Prepare stuffing by gently sauteing onion in melted butter until tender. Combine with cubed bread, tomatoes, basil, salt and pepper to taste. Stuff cavity.
3. Top salmon with remaining lemon and onion slices as well as more dillweed and soft butter on top. Fold and crimp foil tightly. Place on large baking sheet.
4. Preheat oven and bake until thickest part of salmon flakes when prodded with fork, about 45 minutes. Serve warm or chilled.

SEAFOOD STRUDEL

Oven: 375F/190C
Bake: 30 min.
Serves: 4-6

Filo (also known as phyllo) pastry makes an impressive casing for this seafood melange. The paper-thin dough is available fresh from most Greek stores, and frozen from the larger supermarkets about town. The strudel can be completely made ahead and baked last minute. Serve with miniature brioches and a salad.

Crumbs:
2/3	cup fine bread crumbs	150 mL
½	cup freshly grated Parmesan	125 mL
2	tsp. dry mustard	10 mL

Filling:
1	Tbs. butter or margarine	15 mL
½	med. onion, finely minced	½
1½	cups seafood*	375 mL
1	cup dairy sour cream	250 mL
1	med. green onion, chopped	1
2	Tbs. minced parsley	25 mL
½	tsp. salt (or to taste)	2 mL
¼	tsp. pepper	1 mL

Pastry:
4	sheets filo dough	4
1/3	cup melted unsalted butter	75 mL

1. Combine crumb mixture in a small bowl. Set aside.
2. Filling: In a medium skillet, melt butter and gently saute onion. Stir in seafood. Remove from heat and add sour cream, green onion, parsley, and seasonings to taste. Cool.
3. Work with one filo sheet at a time, keeping the remainder covered to prevent from drying out. Lay first sheet on a dry tea towel. Brush top with melted butter. Repeat, stacking each on top of the other. Also butter top sheet.
4. Sprinkle top layer with crumb mixture. Spoon seafood mixture parallel to long edge of sheet, leaving 1 in./2.5 cm margin at the ends.

5. Enclose seafood in pastry by folding in the ends (like envelope). Then brush dough with butter as you roll it. With aid of tea towel, carefully transfer the strudel onto a baking sheet so that the seam faces down. Brush with butter.

6. With a sharp knife, LIGHTLY mark off pastry into 2 in./5 cm segments without cutting through to filling. At this point, strudel may be made ahead and refrigerated.

7. Preheat oven and bake until crisp and golden, about 30 minutes. Let stand briefly for filling to set. Then slice and serve warm.

* You may use any combination of the following: fresh baby shrimp, picked-over crabmeat, sliced raw scallops (well-drained), or poached salmon.

GOLDEN SAUTEED FISH

Fish steaks or fillets
All-purpose flour
Beaten egg with milk
Fine dry bread crumbs
Vegetable oil for pan-frying

Delicious with any kind of fresh fish (salmon, halibut, cod, or sole). Serve with Green Mayonnaise. Leftovers make tasty sandwiches.

1. Dredge fish in flour. Dip in beaten egg-milk mixture. Coat well with crumbs and let "dry" on rack for at least 20 minutes.
2. Heat thin layer of oil in a wide skillet until very hot. Add fish and cook until golden-brown, and flesh is opaque and flakes easily with fork. Turn only once and do not overcook. Sprinkle lightly with salt and pepper. Serve immediately with mayonnaise below.

GREEN MAYONNAISE: Combine ½ cup/125 mL dairy sour cream, ¼ cup/50 mL mayonnaise, 2 tsp./10 mL fresh lemon juice, and ¼ tsp./1 mL salt. Stir in ¼ cup/50 mL EACH of: finely chopped green onion, parsley, and watercress or fresh spinach leaves. Chill thoroughly before using.

EXCELLENT LEG of LAMB

Serves: 4-6

3	lb. (approx.) leg of lamb	1.5 kg
	Salt and pepper	
1	med. clove garlic, slivered	1
	Coating:	
¼	cup Dijon mustard	50 mL
2	Tbs. olive or salad oil	25 mL
2	tsp. soy sauce	10 mL
1	med. clove garlic, minced	1
1	tsp. dried rosemary leaves	5 mL
½	tsp. cracked peppercorns	2 mL
¼	tsp. ground ginger	1 mL

1. Trim off excess fat from leg of lamb. Rub all over with light sprinkling of salt and pepper. Make small gashes in fatty surface and insert a sliver of garlic into each.

2. Combine coating ingredients and brush over entire lamb. Place in shallow roasting pan (may be done ahead and refrigerated, but bring to room temperature before cooking).

3. Preheat oven to 400F/200C. Roast lamb uncovered for 15 minutes. Then reduce heat to 375F/190C and continue roasting for another 45 minutes for medium-rare lamb about 15 min./lb. or 30 min./kg.

4. Let roast stand for 15 minutes before carving. Slice lamb in long thin slabs parallel to leg bone. Serve with hot, de-fatted pan drippings.

Food fanciers will generally agree that lamb is at its best served on the slightly rare side. Those who enjoy their meat well done will love the crispier outside pieces. This lamb is delicious served with its pan juices. Accompany with boiled or roasted potatoes and a roast pepper salad.

SOUVLAKI, TAVERN-STYLE

Broil: 10 min.
Serves: 4-6

2	lb. cubed lamb (from leg)	1 kg
	Marinade:	
1/3	cup good olive oil	75 mL
3	Tbs. fresh lemon juice	50 mL
2	Tbs. grated onion	25 mL
1	lrg. clove garlic, minced	1
1½	tsp. salt	7 mL
1	tsp. crumbled rosemary	5 mL
½	tsp. freshly ground pepper	2 mL

Skewered meat with a Greek touch is perfect for summertime entertaining. Traditional recipes call for lamb; however leg of pork may be successfully substituted here. Souvlaki is very tasty stuffed into pita pockets and topped with a spoonful or two of Tzatziki (yogurt relish).

1. Meat should be cut into 1 in./2.5 cm cubes. Remove all gristle and fat.
2. Combine all marinade ingredients in large mixing bowl. Add cubed lamb, coating well. Let stand in the refrigerator overnight, turning occasionally.
3. If using bamboo skewers, soak them in warm water for several hours before using, otherwise they will burn. Thread meat onto skewers.
4. Broil or barbecue over hot coals for a total of 10 minutes for lamb. Brush with marinade, turning frequently. Do not overcook! Lamb should be slightly pink in the centre.

NOTE: If using pork, cook for a total of 15 minutes or just until pinkness disappears. Pork should be moist, not dry.

TZATZIKI for SOUVLAKI

Serves: 4-6

This yogurt-based vegetable relish has a Mediterranean touch. It is excellent with lamb or anything barbecued. And because tzatziki has a cooling effect, it is an ideal accompaniment to hot, spicy foods.

1	cup unflavoured yogurt	250 mL
1	med. tomato, seeded, chopped	1
1	med. green onion, minced	1
½	sm. cucumber, seeded, chopped	½
1	med. clove garlic, crushed	1
½	tsp. dried dillweed	2 mL

Combine all the above ingredients in small serving bowl. Let stand in refrigerator for 1-2 hours. Remove garlic. Serve as a relish or vegetable side dish.

LOIN of LAMB MONTENEGRO

Oven: 450F/230C
Bake: 15 min.
Serves: 4

Bernie Casavant, head-chef at Jean Pierre's Restaurant in downtown Vancouver is the creator of this superb lamb dish. It received rave reviews from our local food columnists.

2	12 oz. loins of lamb	EA. 350	g
3	slices day-old bread		3
½	cup finely chopped pistachios	125	mL
2	Tbs. minced parsley	25	mL
3	Tbs. olive oil	50	mL
3	Tbs. peanut butter	50	mL
¼	tsp. ground coriander	1	mL
Sauce:			
½	cup lamb or beef stock	125	mL
¼	cup red wine	50	mL
2	Tbs. heavy cream	25	mL
Salt and pepper (to taste)			

1. Trim loins. Pat dry. Season lightly with salt and pepper.
2. Remove crusts from bread. Cube and whirl in processor or finely chop to make fine crumbs. Combine crumbs with chopped pistachios and parsley. Set aside.
3. In wide skillet, heat oil until very hot. Add loins and quickly sear all sides. Remove with slotted spatula and reserve pan.
4. To the peanut butter, mix in coriander. Then spread evenly over top of loins. Roll each in pistachio-crumb mixture to coat completely. Place on baking sheet.
5. Preheat oven. Bake loins until inside of meat is just rose in colour, about 15 minutes. Do not overcook! Keep warm.
6. For sauce, remove grease from reserved pan. Place on heat until it begins to smoke. Remove from heat and add wine to deglaze the pan. Then add the stock. Return pan to heat and boil down, reducing the liquid by one-third.

7. Add the cream and boil until slightly reduced to make a nice sauce. Adjust seasonings to taste. Keep warm.

8. Slice lamb and arrange on warm platters. Pour a little sauce over each serving.

PARMESAN-COATED LAMB CHOPS

Serves: 4

6	fresh lamb chops	6
¼	cup grated Parmesan cheese	50 mL
1	lrg. egg, well-beaten	1
2/3	cup fine bread crumbs	150 mL
	Vegetable oil for cooking	
	Salt and pepper to taste	

For the best of company. Pair this one with a rice pilaf or a baked potato dish. Stuffed tomatoes Provencale make an attractive vegetable accompaniment.

1. Press lamb chops (both sides) in Parmesan. Dip each in beaten egg; then coat in bread crumbs. Let "dry" for at least 30 minutes. May be done ahead and refrigerated, but bring to room temperature before cooking.

2. Heat ¼ in./0.5 cm oil in a wide skillet over medium heat. Add chops without crowding. Cook 2 minutes per side or until nicely browned. Do not overcook! Season lightly with salt and pepper. Serve immediately.

ROAST BRISKET of BEEF

Oven: 350F/180C
Bake: 2-2½ hrs.
Serves: 6

It takes little effort to transform this cheaper cut into a fine-tasting dish. Excellent with roasted or mashed potatoes and your favourite vegetables.

3	lbs. (approx.) brisket of beef	1.5 kg
	Salt and pepper	
	Cooking oil	
1	med. carrot, split lengthwise	1
1	med. tomato, sliced	1
1	rib celery with leaves	1
1	med. onion, thinly sliced	1
½	cup light beef broth	125 mL

1. Sprinkle brisket with salt and pepper. Heat a small amount of oil in a wide skillet. When hot, add meat (fat-side only) to brown, about 10 minutes.

2. Line roasting pan (not too large) with carrot, tomato, and celery. Remove roast and place it brown-side up over top of vegetables in pan.

3. To same skillet in which meat was browned, add the onion slices and slowly saute until light golden. Spoon over top of brisket.

4. Add broth. Cover and roast in preheated oven for about 2 hours until meat is very tender. Cut into thin slices and serve with gravy on the side.

GRAVY: Remove vegetables (onions included) to blender container. Skim off and discard fat from pan juices. Then add to blender to puree. Heat and season to taste.

HUNGARIAN PAPRIKA STEAK

Serves: 4

The best paprika comes from Hungary. It is made from ground chiles and can be "sweet" or "hot", depending on the peppers used. "Sweet" paprika imparts a pleasant, aromatic flavour to this dish. Pair with hot noodles or plain rice.

1½	lbs. sirloin or chuck steak	750 g
4	Tbs. flour (for coating)	60 mL
3	Tbs. cooking oil	50 mL
1	med. onion, chopped	1
1	lrg. clove garlic, minced	1
2	tsp. Hungarian paprika	10 mL
1	cup strong beef broth	250 mL
4	Tbs. tomato paste	60 mL
	Salt and pepper to taste	
	Extras:	
2	med. green peppers, in strips	2
2	med. red peppers, in strips	2

1. Pound meat to ¼ in./0.5 cm thickness. Cut into smaller serving pieces. Coat well with flour. Set aside.
2. Heat oil in large skillet using medium heat setting. Brown meat in two separate batches. Remove and set aside.
3. To same pan, add onion, garlic, and if necessary, more oil. Saute until tender. Stir in paprika and cook briefly.
4. Add broth and tomato paste, scraping up brown bits from bottom. Return beef and accumulated juices. Simmer covered over low heat until tender, about 40 minutes. Season. May be made ahead and reheated.
5. Just before serving time, add bell pepper strips. Cook, stirring until heated through. Serve immediately.

CARBONNADE of BEEF
(Beef and Onions in Beer)

Oven: 325F/160C
Bake: 2 hrs.
Serves: 4-6

A beery beef stew made famous by the Belgians. Look for a good buy on chuck roast (1.5 kg at least to accommodate for wastage) and cut it yourself. A winner with hot buttered noodles and steamed carrots.

2½	lbs. stew-size pieces of chuck	1 kg
4	Tbs. all-purpose flour	60 mL
2	Tbs. vegetable oil (or more)	25 mL
4	Tbs. butter or margarine	60 mL
4	med. onions, thinly sliced	4
2	lrg. cloves garlic, minced	2
2	tsp. brown sugar	10 mL
1	tin beef broth, undiluted	284 mL
1	bottle dark or regular beer	341 mL
2	Tbs. red wine vinegar	25 mL
2	med. bay leaves	2
1	tsp. crumbled thyme leaves	5 mL
½	tsp salt (or to taste)	2 mL
½	tsp. freshly ground pepper	2 mL
2	Tbs. minced parsley (garnish)	25 mL

1. Dust cubes of beef with flour. Heat oil in heavy skillet and brown meat in 2-3 separate batches. Remove with slotted spoon to large heatproof casserole.
2. To the same skillet, add butter and slowly cook onions until tender and carmelized (not burned). Stir in garlic. Then sprinkle in sugar and any leftover flour.
3. Add broth, beer, vinegar, the herbs, and seasonings. Mix well to blend. Pour over meat in casserole. Cover tightly.
4. Preheat oven. Cook stew for about 2 hours or until meat is tender. May be completely made ahead and rewarmed. Skim off fat. Sprinkle with parsley before serving.

BEEF and POTATO COMBO

Serves: 4

Serving a potato dish with rice may sound a bit excessive; but here, the two do surprisingly complement one another. This is a childhood favourite, one which my Dad frequently stirred up for the family. It's a good meal-stretcher. My kids even love it.

¾	lb. flank steak, thinly sliced	350 g
	Marinade:	
1	Tbs. dark soya sauce	15 mL
2	tsp. water or sherry	10 mL
2	tsp. cornstarch	10 mL
1	tsp. finely minced ginger root	5 mL
½	tsp. salt (or to taste)	2 mL
	Extras:	
2	Tbs. corn or peanut oil	25 mL
1	lrg. clove garlic, crushed	1
6	green onions, in 2 in./5 cm slices	6
6	med. potatoes, peeled, sliced	6
1	cup light beef broth	250 mL

1. Combine beef with marinade ingredients. Mix well and let stand 15-20 minutes at room temperature.

2. In a wok or heavy skillet over high heat, add oil until sizzling hot. Add garlic, quickly sauteing to brown (do not burn).

3. Add beef strips and green onions, stirring and flipping constantly for 1-2 minutes. Remove to platter and set aside.

4. To same skillet, add the potatoes and broth, scraping up brown bits from bottom of pan. Bring to a boil. Cover and reduce heat to low simmer. Check for liquid, adding more broth if required.

5. Cook potatoes until very tender; but not falling apart, about 15 minutes. Return beef mixture, stirring gently to heat through. Taste for seasonings. Serve with a pot of steaming rice. Good!

FRIKADELLER
(Danish Meat Patties)

Makes: 10

Every Danish family's favourite. These are soo-oo good, you'll get asked time and again to make them. Special thanks go to my good friend, Elin for sharing this recipe with us. Serve with boiled or mashed potatoes and braised red cabbage or Agurkesalat, a tangy cucumber salad. Will serve 4 nicely.

½	lb. ground veal	250 g
½	lb. ground pork	250 g
1	sm. onion, finely minced	1
1	lrg. egg, beaten	1
½	tsp. salt	2 mL
¼	tsp. pepper	1 mL
½	cup club soda	125 mL
3	Tbs. all-purpose flour	50 mL
Extras:		
4	Tbs. butter or margarine	50 mL
2	Tbs. vegetable oil	25 mL
½	cup stock or broth	125 mL
½	cup heavy cream	125 mL
2	Tbs. minced parsley	25 mL

1. In large mixing bowl, combine veal, pork, onion, egg, salt and pepper. Mix well.
2. In a small bowl, gradually add club soda to the flour to form a thin paste. Add this to meat mixture, beating thoroughly until light and fluffy.
3. Cover tightly and refrigerate several hours until slightly firmed.
4. To cook, heat butter and oil together in a wide, heavy skillet. With a tablespoon, form and shape mixture against inside of bowl into ovals, about 2 in./5 cm long and 1 in./2.5 cm thick. Add patties to hot pan and cook about 5 minutes per side until golden-brown.
5. Remove patties from pan. Drain off excess oil. Add stock to pan and scrape up all the brown bits.
6. Return patties. Cover and simmer on low heat for about 30 minutes. Just before serving, add cream and lots of parsley. Serve hot.

BAKED STUFFED RIBS

Oven: 350F/180C
Bake: 1½ hrs.
Serves: 4

Mostly bone and little meat, ribs are generally considered a treat rather than a bargain buy. Here is a delicious way of stretching out a good thing. If you can buy back ribs on special, they are the best — a lot leaner and tender than the regular side ribs, and the perfect vehicle for stuffing. Side ribs are best briefly parboiled to tenderize and remove unwanted fat.

3	med. slabs pork back ribs, about	1.5 kg
	Cooking oil — Salt and pepper	
	Stuffing:	
6	cups finely cubed bread	1.5 L
⅓	cup butter or margarine	75 mL
1	med. onion, finely chopped	1
2	med. ribs celery, chopped	2
2	Tbs. minced parsley	25 mL
1	tsp. savory or poultry seasoning	5 mL
¼	tsp. salt (or to taste)	1 mL
2	med. tart apples, pared, chopped	2
1	cup golden raisins, plumped	250 mL
½	cup light broth or water	125 mL

1. Divide meat into 8 equal segments to allow each serving two portions with a generous amount of stuffing to be "sandwiched" in between. Rub the meat with oil and a light sprinkling of salt and pepper.

2. For stuffing, place cubed bread in the largest mixing bowl you can find. Set aside. Melt butter in a large skillet. Add onion, celery, and parsley, gently sauteing until tender. Add seasonings.

3. Pour mixture over bread cubes in bowl. Add apples, raisins, and broth (just to moisten), mixing with hands until well incorporated. Taste for seasonings. Form 4 balls.

4. Spread the bone-side of 4 rib portions with ball of stuffing. "Sandwich" with remaining meat pieces. Tie if desired, but I do not find this necessary.

5. Place stuffed ribs on small foil-lined baking sheet. Bake in preheated oven, uncovered for 1 hour. Then cover lightly with foil and bake an additional 30 minutes until meat is very tender.

INDONESIAN-STYLE SATE

Grill: 15 min.
Serves: 4-6

Sate, skewered spicy meat is perhaps the best known of all south-east Asian dishes. This recipe is close to an authentic version which I adapted from an Indonesian cookbook. Serve with fried rice and long spears of seedless cucumber.

2	lbs. lean pork cubes*	1 kg
2	med. onions, crushed	2
6	wooden skewers, soaked	6
	Salad oil for drizzling	
	Marinade:	
6	**Brazil nuts, finely grated**	6
¼	**cup Ketjap or soya sauce**	50 mL
3	**lrg cloves garlic, crushed**	3
2	**Tbs. brown sugar**	25 mL
2	**Tbs. fresh lemon juice**	25 mL
2	**Tbs. dry sherry**	25 mL
2	**Tbs. salad oil**	25 mL
2	**tsp. salt**	10 mL
2	**tsp. ground coriander**	10 mL
1	**tsp. ground cumin seed**	5 mL
½	**tsp. crumbled dried chiles**	2 mL
½	**tsp. pepper**	2 mL

1. In large stainless or glass mixing bowl, stir together marinade ingredients until well-blended. Add meat rubbing in the sauce with hands. Add crushed onions. Cover. Let stand for at least 8 hours or overnight in the refrigerator.
2. Thread the meat onto skewers which have been soaked for several hours. Let meat stand at room temperature for 1 hour prior to barbequeing.
3. Drizzle meat with a little salad oil. Broil over hot coals, turning often until nicely browned — about 15 minutes. Do not overcook; otherwise sate will be dry.

4. Before eating, it is good manners to say, "Selamat Makan", meaning "Enjoy your meal"; or "Have a blessed meal".

*NOTE: Chicken beef, and lamb will require only 10 minutes cooking time.

LEMON HONEY SPARERIBS

Oven: 325F/160C
Bake: 2 hrs.
Serves: 4

A "Wong" favourite from my friend, Deanna. Serve with plain steamed rice and stir-fried veggies.

1	lrg. rack pork spareribs	2 kg
	Flour — Cooking Oil	
	Sauce:	
½	cup honey	125 mL
2	med. lemons, for juice	2
1	tsp. salt	5 mL
½	tsp. garlic powder	2 mL

1. Cut meat into 2-rib portions. Roll in flour and brown in a little hot oil, a few pieces at a time. When all are browned, transfer to shallow roasting pan and arrange in a single layer.
2. Mix sauce ingredients and pour over meat. Cover lightly with foil and bake in preheated oven for about 2 hours or until golden and tender. Baste several times during cooking. Serve hot.

SAVORY HAM LOAF

Oven: 350F/180C
Bake: 1½ hrs.
Serves: 8-10

Convert that leftover ham into a delectable meat loaf that can be served either hot or cold. The glaze is optional, but does add a flavorful piquant touch.

4	cups coarsely ground ham	1 L
1	lb. ground raw pork	500 g
2	lrg. eggs	2
1	sm. onion, minced	1
1	cup soda cracker crumbs	250 mL
1	cup milk	250 mL
1	tsp. dry mustard	5 mL
½	tsp. salt	2 mL
¼	tsp. pepper	1 mL
	Glaze:	
⅓	cup packed brown sugar	75 mL
1	Tbs. prepared mustard	15 mL
1	Tbs. cider vinegar	15 mL

1. Combine above meatloaf ingredients. Mix well. Pack into 9x5 in./2 L loaf pan.
2. Preheat oven and bake for 1 hour. Combine glaze mixture and spoon over top of loaf. Continue baking for an additional 30 minutes. Meatloaf is cooked when it shrinks away from sides of pan.
3. Cool slightly before serving. Delicious with mashed potatoes, potatoes, or potato salad.

MAHOGANY WINGS

Broil: 16-18 min.
Serves: 4-6

Finger-licking good! Anise, a licorice flavoured, star-shaped seed gives these wings a most delicious lift. Good served as part of a Chinese menu.

2	lb. chicken wings	1 kg
¾	cup water	175 mL
1	med. 5-star anise	1
½	cup medium soy sauce	125 mL
½	cup brown sugar	125 mL
1	med. slice ginger, mashed	1
2	tsp. dry sherry	10 mL
½	tsp. salt (or to taste)	2 mL

1. Rinse and pat chicken wings dry. Fold back wing tips.
2. In a large stainless saucepan, bring water with star anise to a boil. Let simmer 10 minutes. Remove anise.
3. Add remaining ingredients and let mixture come to a boil. Add chicken wings, only as many as liquid will accommodate (two batches may be necessary). Cover and cook for 10 minutes.
4. Meanwhile line baking sheet with foil. Lift wings from liquid using tongs. Set on foil-lined pan. May be done ahead.
5. Just before serving time, preheat oven broiler. Set pan 4 in./10 cm from heat source and brown wings, about 8 minutes per side. Delicious warm or cold. Serviettes required.

NOTE: The soy mixture may be stored in a jar and refrigerated for up to 2 weeks to re-use. Star anise may be found in the spice department.

BARBEQUED GINGER CHICKEN

Oven: 450F/230C
Bake: 45 min.
Serves: 4-6

I like this one. It was another tasty offering that appeared on Trader Vic's "California Native Foods" menu. A blender is not necessary, but does simplify the job. It also turns out a smoother and I think, more flavourful sauce. Thanks to manager, Jackson Lew.

2	sm. fryers, cut in half	2
	Sauce:	
½	cup tomato chili sauce	125 mL
⅓	cup soy sauce	75 mL
⅓	cup dry sherry	75 mL
⅓	cup salad oil	75 mL
¼	cup brown sugar	50 mL
2	Tbs. chopped ginger root	25 mL
2	lrg. cloves garlic, minced	2
1	tsp. tabasco sauce (or more)	5 mL
1	tsp. pepper	5 mL
½	tsp. salt	2 mL

1. Pat chicken halves dry and place in a large mixing bowl.
2. Combine sauce ingredients (blender is excellent) and mix until smooth. Pour over chicken, coating well. Cover and refrigerate overnight. Turn occasionally.
3. Preheat oven. Bake about 45 minutes or until juices run clear. Baste throughout cooking until nicely glazed.

FOR BARBEQUE GRILLING: Do not brush sauce onto chicken until last few minutes of cooking, otherwise you will have a scorched mess! In this case, the sauce will coat up to 4 fryers, each cut in half.

CHICKEN with SUN-DRIED TOMATOES

Serves: 4

4	single chicken breasts	4
3	Tbs. butter or margarine	50 mL
1	lrg. shallot, minced	1
¾	cup heavy cream	175 mL
½	cup dry white wine	125 mL
3	Tbs. chopped pumate	50 mL
¼	tsp. dried dillweed	1 mL
	Salt and pepper to taste	

1. Skin and debone chicken breasts. Slice each piece crosswise on the diagonal into 6 portions.
2. In wide stainless skillet over medium heat, melt butter and saute chicken pieces just until pinkness disappears, about 3 minutes. Remove chicken to platter.
3. To the same skillet, add shallot and stir for about 5 minutes. Add cream, wine, sun-dried tomatoes, and dillweed. Bring to a boil, cooking and stirring until liquid is reduced to a nice, medium-thick sauce (about 8 minutes).
4. Add chicken and let simmer gently for a couple of minutes just until heated through. Season to taste. Serve immediately.

Pumate, also known as sun-dried tomatoes are generally found in Italian specialty shops and sometimes the larger pasta outlets. A little goes a long way, so don't buy out the store. Accompany this dynamic-tasting dish with boiled spring potatoes, steamed asparagus, and a sprightly bouquet of watercress.

HONEY-GARLIC BAKED CHICKEN

Oven: 350F/180C
Bake: 45 min.
Serves: 4-6

One of those recipes everybody asks for...

1	lrg. fryer chicken, cut-up	1.5 kg
	Sauce:	
½	cup honey	125 mL
¼	cup soya sauce	50 mL
2	Tbs. corn oil	25 mL
4	med. cloves garlic, crushed	4
1	tsp. grated ginger root	5 mL
½	tsp. salt	2 mL

1. Pat chicken pieces dry. Place skin-side down in wide shallow baking dish, in single layer.
2. Combine sauce ingredients in small saucepan. Bring to a boil. Reduce heat to low and let mixture simmer gently for 10 minutes. May be made ahead and stored in a glass jar.
3. Pour the mixture over chicken, coating well. May be done ahead, but keep refrigerated. Bake in preheated oven turning and basting until chicken is nicely browned and sauce is slightly syrupy. Chicken is cooked when juices run clear.
4. Serve chicken with sauce spooned over. Delicious hot or cold, with steamed rice.

NOTE: This honey-garlic glaze makes an excellent basting sauce for whole turkey. Brush mixture onto turkey during last 1 hour of roasting, about every 15 minutes until nicely browned. For turkey or chicken pieces over the barbeque, baste last 15 minutes of cooking time (not much sooner or glaze will burn).

SIMPLY SUPER ROAST CHICKEN

Oven: 400F/200C
Bake: 1 hr.
Serves: 4

1	lrg. chicken fryer	1.5 kg
1	med. lemon, halved	1
½	tsp. salt (in cavity)	2 mL
2	lrg. green onions	2
	Vegetable oil	
	Salt and pepper	

1. Preheat oven. Pat chicken dry, cavity included. Rub all over with squeezed lemon (save cores). Sprinkle inside with salt and then stuff with lemon cores and whole green onions.
2. Skewer cavity closed. Rub the outside with vegetable oil and place chicken in lightly-oiled wok or on rack in shallow roasting pan.
3. Roast breast-side DOWN for the first 20 minutes. Baste. Then turn chicken breast-side UP for the remainder of the cooking time, 40-45 minutes or until chicken is nicely browned and juices run clear from leg joint.
4. Sprinkle with salt and pepper. Let chicken rest at room temperature 15-20 minutes for juices to set. Serve warm or chilled, delicious either way.

NOTE: Did you know that a wok makes one of the best "vehicles" for roasting chicken? It's just the right shape and the right size, and conducts about the right amount of heat.

I think that many of us have forgotten just how good a plain roasted chicken can taste. My family loves it with mashed potatoes and dribbles of gravy. Leftovers? Never a problem. Simply convert them to sandwiches, salads, soups, and casseroles.

DUCK with BLUEBERRIES "RICHMOND"

Serves: 4

2	plump ducklings	EA. approx.	1.5 kg
	Salt and pepper		
	Sauce:		
¾	cup red wine vinegar		200 mL
2	Tbs. butter		25 mL
½	cup granulated sugar		125 mL
4	med. oranges, for juice		4
⅓	cup brown stock or gravy		75 mL
¼	cup fresh/frozen blueberries		50 mL
	Dash cognac (to taste)		

One of the most popular dishes featured at Bruno Marti's La Belle Auberge in Ladner, B.C. It's easy, elegant, and delicious; but does require preparation time. Bruno, one of the five members of Team Canada was bestowed top honours at the 1984 World Culinary Olympics in Frankfurt, W. Germany.

1. Season ducks with salt and pepper. Roast at 500F/250C for 30 minutes. Reduce heat to 350F/180C and roast for another 1 hour, basting twice with pan drippings. Allow to cool while making sauce.
2. Boil vinegar in small stainless pan until it has been reduced to 2 Tbs./25 mL. In a larger saucepan, heat butter and sugar together over medium heat until mixture carmelizes into a golden-brown syrup (watch carefully).
3. Add the reduced vinegar, orange juice, and stock, stirring until carmel has dissolved. Then boil until reduced down to a nice sauce that coats wooden spoon. Add berries and cognac. Keep warm.
4. Carve duck and arrange on warm platter(s). Spoon sauce over and serve with white rice, green beans, and cubed, peeled tomatoes (or vegetables to your liking). Pass extra sauce separately.

GOLDEN ROAST GOOSE

Serves: 6

8-10	lb. fresh young goose	4-5 kg
	Salt and pepper	
1	onion, studded with cloves	1
1	lrg. apple, peeled, quartered	1
1	cup water (for pan)	250 mL

Make goose the feature attraction for your next Christmas dinner. We did, and what an applause it received. Serve with a fruit or chestnut stuffing, cooked separately from the bird. The following preparation is best for a fresh goose weighing no more than 10 pounds.

1. Preheat oven to 425F/220C. Remove neck, liver, and giblets from cavity. Also remove excess fat (reserve and render for other purposes).
2. Wipe goose with damp cloth and prick skin (not too deeply) all over. Rub inside and out with salt and pepper.
3. Stuff cavity with onion and apple. Skewer or sew cavity closed. Place breast-side up on rack placed in shallow roasting pan. Add water to bottom of pan to stop fat from splattering all over.
4. Cook uncovered for 30 minutes at high heat. Then reduce oven to 350F/180C and continue roasting 25 min. per lb./50 min. per kg including initial cooking, until goose is a beautiful golden-brown. Juices around thigh area should run beige, not pink when lightly pricked. Baste occasionally.
5. Let goose rest a good 20 minutes before carving. Discard onion and apple as they will be too fatty to serve.

TURKEY-IN-THE-STEW

Serves: 4

Round out this economical meal-in-one with a warm crusty loaf from your favourite bakery. Turkey stewing meat is available at specialty meat shops; but failing that, substitute cubed lean pork. It's surprisingly tasty.

1½	lbs. turkey stew meat	750 g
4	Tbs. flour for coating	50 mL
3	Tbs. cooking oil	50 mL
1	med. onion, chopped	1
2	lrg. carrots, in chunks	2
2	cups light chicken broth	500 mL
1	tsp. crumbled thyme leaves	5 mL
2	lrg. potatoes, in chunks	2
1	cup frozen peas	250 mL
	Salt and pepper to taste	

1. Cut meat into 1.5 in./4 cm pieces. Lightly dredge with flour.
2. Heat oil in a large, heavy pot and brown turkey in two separate batches. Remove to platter and set aside.
3. To the same pot, add onion and briefly cook. Add carrots, broth and thyme, scraping up brown bits from bottom of pot. Return turkey and let come to a boil. Reduce heat to low and cover.
4. Let simmer gently for 30 minutes. Then add potatoes. Cook an additional 25-30 minutes until everything is tender. To retain the nice green colour of the peas, add them just before serving time. Season stew with salt and pepper.

BREADS

SUNDAY MORNING PANCAKES

Makes: 12

These old-fashioned pancakes really are delicious, fluffy, and moist. The wheat germ adds extra flavour and nutrition, making them an all round Sunday favourite. Good with whipped butter and real maple syrup or blueberry-lemon sauce. Feeds 4 only!

Mixture 1:

2	cups all-purpose flour	500 mL
¼	cup wheat germ	50 mL
2	Tbs. granulated sugar	25 mL
2	tsp. baking powder	10 mL
1	tsp. baking soda	5 mL
½	tsp. salt	2 mL

Mixture 2:

2	cups buttermilk*	500 mL
2	lrg. eggs	2
¼	cup corn oil	50 mL

1. In medium mixing bowl, stir together all dry ingredients with whisk. Mix well.
2. In large mixing bowl, beat buttermilk, eggs, and corn oil. Add dry mixture, stirring ONLY until moistened. Do not overmix! Batter will be lumpy. If too thick, stir in a little milk.
3. Measure about 1/3 cup/75 mL batter for each hotcake. Place on hot, greased griddle or electric frying pan using medium-high setting.
4. Flip over after tops are bubbly and slightly dry. Cook until other sides are nicely browned.

* Substitute soured milk. To 2 cups/500 mL fresh milk, add 2 Tbs./25 mL white vinegar. Stir. Let stand 10 minutes to curdle.

SWEDISH OATMEAL PANCAKES

Serves: 4

Swedish pancakes are traditionally served with lingonberry sauce, however you'll find maple syrup also very good. This batter requires at least 30 minutes standing time.

Mixture 1:
2	cups regular rolled oats	500 mL
½	cup all-purpose flour	125 mL
2	Tbs. granulated sugar	25 mL
1	tsp. baking powder	5 mL
1	tsp. baking soda	5 mL
¼	tsp. salt	1 mL

Mixture 2:
2	cups buttermilk	500 mL
2	lrg. eggs, beaten	2
¼	cup butter, melted	50 mL
1	tsp. vanilla	5 mL
	Oil for griddle	

1. In medium mixing bowl, combine all the dry ingredients. Stir well with whisk and set aside.

2. In larger bowl, beat together all ingredients in Mixture 2. Add dry mixture, mixing with wooden spoon JUST until moistened. Do not beat or overmix! Let stand 30-45 minutes. Batter will thicken.

3. Heat griddle or skillet over medium heat. Grease. Use a scant ¼ cup/50 mL batter for each pancake. Cook until tiny bubbles form on top. Flip over and brown. Serve hot.

SPECTACULAR APPLE PANCAKE

Oven: 425F/220C
Bake: 25 min.
Serves: 4

This is a very delicious oven-baked pancake. And quite spectacular as well. It puffs up to twice its volume and like a souffle, must be served immediately. Present this one with oven-baked breakfast sausages and some fresh fruit on the side.

4	med. apples	4
2	Tbs. fresh lemon juice	25 mL
3	Tbs. granulated sugar	50 mL
½	tsp. cinnamon	2 mL
2	Tbs. butter or margarine	25 mL
Batter:		
4	lrg. eggs, room temperature	4
1	cup milk	250 mL
1	cup all-purpose flour	250 mL
¼	tsp. salt	1 mL
Glaze:		
2	Tbs. butter or margarine	25 mL
¼	cup brown sugar	50 mL
½	tsp. cinnamon (opt.)	2 mL

1. Preheat oven. Peel and slice apples. Toss with lemon juice. Then add sugar and cinnamon.
2. In a 10 in./25 cm skillet with oven-proof handle (cast iron is excellent), melt the butter and add apple mixture to saute until golden and tender, about 8 minutes. Do not overcook.
3. While apples are cooking, prepare the batter. Beat eggs in large mixing bowl. Gradually beat in milk, and then the flour and salt until smooth.
4. Pour batter over hot apples in skillet and immediately transfer the whole thing to hot oven. Bake until puffed and golden-brown.
5. While pancake is baking, make the topping. In a small saucepan, melt butter and mix in brown sugar and cinnamon. Set aside.

6. When baking time is up, switch oven setting to broil. Drizzle glaze all over pancake and let the top crispen and brown. Watch very carefully, as this will happen right before your eyes.

7. Using hot mats, parade to the table and serve straight from the skillet.

BLUEBERRY-LEMON SAUCE

Cook: 2-3 min.
Makes: 2 cups/500 mL

2	cups fresh or frozen blueberries	500 mL
1/3	cup granulated sugar	75 mL
1/4	cup water	50 mL
1	sm. lemon, rind and juice	1
	Thickener:	
2	tsp. cornstarch	10 mL
1	Tbs. water	15 mL

Have you ever tried wild blueberries? They add a real burst of flavour to this easy-to-make sauce. Heavenly spooned over pancakes.

Combine berries, sugar, water, lemon rind, and juice in a saucepan. Bring to a gentle boil. Mix together paste of cornstarch and water. Add, stirring constantly until sauce is translucent and thickened, 2-3 minutes. Keep warm over pan of hot water.

BLUEBERRY STREUSEL MUFFINS

Oven: 425F/220C
Bake: 20-25 min.
Yields: 12 lrg.

Chockful of blueberries with a sugar-cinnamon topping. Mm-mm.

Mixture 1:

2½	cups all-purpose flour	625 mL
1	Tbs. baking powder	15 mL
½	tsp. baking soda	2 mL
½	tsp. salt	2 mL

Mixture 2:

2	lrg. eggs, room temperature	2
¾	cup granulated sugar	175 mL
½	cup vegetable oil	125 mL
1	lrg. orange, rind & juice	1
1	cup yogurt or sour cream	250 mL

Extras:

2	cups fresh or frozen blueberries	500 mL
	Streusel Topping (below)	

1. Preheat oven and generously grease muffin tins. Make streusel topping and set aside.
2. Combine dry ingredients in a medium bowl, stirring well with whisk.
3. In larger bowl, beat together eggs, sugar, and oil until smooth and well-blended. Mix in orange rind and juice along with sour cream.
4. Add flour mixture, mixing with wooden spoon just until moistened. Quickly, but gently fold in berries. Do not overmix!
5. Spoon batter into prepared tins, filling to the very top. Sprinkle with streusel. Pop into oven and bake until golden-brown. Toothpick inserted into muffin should come out clean.

STREUSEL TOPPING: Combine ¼ cup/50 mL granulated sugar, 3 Tbs./50 mL all-purpose flour, and ½ tsp./2 mL cinnamon. Cut in 2 Tbs./25 mL chilled butter until mixture resembles fine crumbs.

CHUNKY DATE BRAN MUFFINS

Oven: 400F/200C
Bake: 20-25 min.
Yields: 18 lrg.

Rewarmed for a split second in the microwave, these fibre rich muffins make a most satisfying early morning treat. Dates, walnuts, and orange zest provide the reinforcing touch to make these a favourite with the whole family. No eggs here; but if you wish, you may add a large one to the oil-sugar mixture.

Mixture 1:
3	cups natural bran	750 mL
1½	cups all-purpose flour	375 mL
⅓	cup wheat germ	75 mL
2	tsp. baking soda	10 mL
1	tsp. baking powder	5 mL
½	tsp. salt	2 mL
1½	cups chopped pitted dates*	375 mL
1	cup chopped walnuts	250 mL
1	Tbs. grated orange rind	15 mL

Mixture 2:
½	cup vegetable oil	125 mL
½	cup molasses	125 mL
⅓	cup brown sugar, packed	75 mL
2½	cups buttermilk	625 mL

1. Preheat oven. Grease muffin tins.
2. In medium mixing bowl, combine bran, flour, wheat germ, baking soda, baking powder, and salt. Mix in dates, nuts, and rind.
3. In large bowl, beat together oil, molasses, and brown sugar until well blended. Mix in buttermilk.
4. Add dry mixture, stirring with wooden spoon just until moistened. Do not beat or overmix!
5. Fill each muffin tin to the very top. Bake in preheated oven until nicely browned. Toothpick inserted in centre should come out clean. Serve warm.

* Try chopped pitted prunes or raisins instead.

ISLAND BANANA MUFFINS

Oven: 400F/200C
Bake: 25 min.
Yields: 12-14

Exceptional! Use speckled bananas for the best flavour.

Mixture 1:
2	cups all-purpose flour	500 mL
¼	cup wheat germ	50 mL
1	tsp. baking soda	5 mL
1	tsp. baking powder	5 mL
½	tsp. salt	2 mL
1	cup chopped walnuts*	250 mL

Mixture 2:
3	lrg. very ripe bananas	3
2	lrg. eggs, room temperature	2
¾	cup granulated sugar	175 mL
½	cup vegetable oil	125 mL
½	cup buttermilk	125 mL
1	tsp. vanilla	5 mL

1. Preheat oven. Grease muffin tins.
2. In medium mixing bowl, combine flour, wheat germ, baking soda, baking powder, and salt. Mix well with whisk. Stir in nuts. Set aside.
3. In larger bowl, mash bananas to make 1½ cups/375 mL. Beat in eggs, sugar, oil, buttermilk, and vanilla until smooth and well blended.
4. Add flour mixture, stirring with wooden spoon only until moistened. Do not beat or overmix!
5. Spoon batter to the very top of prepared tins. Bake in preheated oven until nicely browned. Toothpick inserted in centre should come out clean.

* VARIATION: Try chopped dried apricots. Chocolate chips are good, too.

PEBBLE-TOP SODA BREAD

Oven: 375F/190C
Bake: 1 hr.
Yields: 1 loaf

A "round" of this quick bread makes a very nice accompaniment to soups and stews. We especially like it served warm, in thick slices with butter and honey or marmalade.

2	cups wholewheat flour	500 mL
2	cups all-purpose flour	500 mL
2	Tbs. brown sugar	25 mL
1	Tbs. baking powder	15 mL
1	tsp. baking soda	5 mL
1	tsp. salt	5 mL
¼	cup chilled butter	50 mL
1¾	cups buttermilk	425 mL
1	lrg. egg, beaten	1
⅓	cup large oat flakes	75 mL

1. Preheat oven. In a large mixing bowl, combine both flours, sugar, baking powder and soda, and the salt using a whisk to mix. Cut in butter using 2 knives or a pastry blender until mixture resembles coarse crumbs.

2. In a separate bowl, combine buttermilk and egg. Add to the crumbly mixture, stirring with wooden spoon ONLY until blended. Do not beat or overmix! Knead briefly, about 10 strokes.

3. Spread large flakes of oats on table and press dough into it to coat. Shape into a large ball. Place on greased sheet. Flatten slightly. With a sharp knife, cut cross-wise slashes on top. Bake in preheated oven for about 1 hour or until loaf sounds hollow when tapped.

RAISIN-BUTTERMILK SCRUMPETS

Oven: 425F/220C
Bake: 12-15 min.
Yields: 10-12

Accurate measuring plus a light hand will ensure excellent results here. These gigantic scones take only minutes to make. Try them — and be ready for the rants and raves.

3	cups all-purpose flour	750 mL
1	Tbs. baking powder	15 mL
1	tsp. baking soda	5 mL
½	tsp. salt	2 mL
⅓	cup granulated sugar	75 mL
¼	cup chilled butter	50 mL
¼	cup chilled shortening	50 mL
1	cup raisins or currants	250 mL
2	lrg. eggs, room temperature	2
¾	cup buttermilk	175 mL

1. Preheat oven. In a large mixing bowl, combine flour, baking powder, soda, salt, and sugar. Mix well with whisk.
2. Cut in butter and shortening with pastry blender or two knives until mixture resembles coarse crumbs. Mix in raisins. Make a well in the centre.
3. With fork, lightly beat eggs with buttermilk and pour into well. Stir quickly just until everything is moistened. Knead gently 6-8 turns. Transfer to floured surface.
4. Pat or roll gently to ½ in./1.5 cm thickness. Cut into rounds with empty tuna tin. Place on ungreased baking sheet and bake about 12 minutes or until golden-brown. Best served hot.

WELSH CAKES (SCONES)

Oven: 350F/180C
Bake: 25 min.
Yields: 24-36

2	cups all-purpose flour	500 mL
1	cup graham flour*	250 mL
1½	tsp. baking powder	7 mL
1	tsp. nutmeg	5 mL
½	tsp. baking soda	2 mL
½	cup brown sugar	125 mL
⅔	cup lard	150 mL
⅓	cup margarine	75 mL
1	cup currants	250 mL
2	lrg. eggs	2
⅓	cup milk (maybe more)	75 mL

These tasty currant "affairs" once sustained free-lance librarian, Kathleen Nichol and a friend for a week of lunches on their cross-Canada car journey. From Kathleen's book, "A Batch of Biscuits", published by Bottesini Press of Vancouver.

1. In large mixing bowl, combine all-purpose flour, graham flour, baking powder, nutmeg, baking soda, and brown sugar. Using pastry blender or 2 knives, cut in lard and margarine till crumbly. Stir in currants.
2. In separate bowl, beat eggs and milk. Add to the flour mixture using more milk if necessary to make a soft dough. Do not overmix! Knead lightly and gently on floured surface — just a few strokes.
3. Roll out dough to ½ in./1 cm thickness. Cut into rounds with cookie cutter or rim of small tumbler. Place on ungreased baking sheet(s).
4. Bake in preheated oven for about 25 minutes or on a heated griddle at 350F/180C for 10-12 minutes per side until nicely browned and heated through. Cool on wire rack.

* Graham flour is similar to wholewheat flour, but with a higher bran content. You may substitute all-purpose flour plus some bran or wheat germ or wholewheat.

STICKY CINNAMON BUNS

Oven: 375F/190C
Bake: 25-30 min.
Yields: 15-16

Gooey 'n good! These gigantic yeast-risen swirls of cinnamon, raisin, and a light coating of caramel are sure to become a favourite with family and friends. Not difficult to make, but they do need time.

Yeast:
½	cup lukewarm water	125 mL
	Pinch granulated sugar	
1	Tbs. active dry yeast	15 mL

Dough:
1	cup milk, scalded	250 mL
⅓	cup vegetable shortening	75 mL
2	Tbs. granulated sugar	25 mL
2	tsp. salt	10 mL
1	cup cold water	250 mL
2	lrg. eggs, beaten	2
6	cups all-purpose flour	1.5 L

Goodies:
¼	cup soft butter or margarine	50 mL
½	cup brown sugar	125 mL
2	tsp. cinnamon	10 mL
1½	cups raisins, plumped	375 mL

1. In a very large mixing bowl, combine lukewarm water with sugar. Sprinkle yeast on top and let soften 10 minutes.
2. Meanwhile, scald milk by heating it in a saucepan just until tiny bubbles form around edges. Add shortening to melt.
3. Remove from heat and stir in sugar and salt. Mix in cold water and beaten eggs. Add softened yeast and stir well.
4. Beat in ONLY 4 cups/1 L of the flour. Add remaining 2 cups/500 mL (may need more), mixing with hands until a soft, non-sticky dough forms. Turn out onto lightly-floured surface and knead 5 minutes.

5. Grease ball of dough and place back into large bowl. Cover with towel and set in warm place to rise until double in bulk, about 1½ hours. If room is cool, set bowl of dough over pan of hot tap water.

6. Meanwhile, combine syrup ingredients (below) and spread evenly over bottom of large, shallow well-greased pan or roaster with 2 in./5 cm high sides (important as buns will rise and syrup otherwise flow over).

7. Punch down dough. Roll and stretch out onto floured surface into 12 x 24 in./30 x 60 cm rectangle. Slather top with soft butter. Sprinkle with mixture of brown sugar and cinnamon, and then top with drained, plumped raisins.

8. Starting at one of the long ends, roll up dough into long cylinder, like jelly roll. Pinch edges together. Mark into 15-16 segments and then slice with sharp knife.

9. Arrange slices in pan over caramel. Poke raisins back into dough as they tend to burn. Cover and let rise for an additional 45 minutes or until double in bulk.

10. Preheat oven. Bake about 25 minutes or until golden brown. Immediately (and carefully), invert buns onto large sheet of heavy duty foil so that syrup will dribble into buns. Cool slightly before serving. Best eaten same day as they are made.

CARAMEL SYRUP: Melt ½ cup/125 mL butter or margarine. Stir in 1 cup/250 mL brown sugar and 2 Tbs. corn syrup until well blended.

RAISIN PUMPERNICKEL ROUNDS

Oven: 375F/190C
Bake: 50-55 min.
Yields: 2 rounds

This delicious dark bread is made with three types of flour: rye, wholewheat, and unbleached white...plus a lot of raisins to give it a touch of California sunshine. Its sturdy goodness makes it perfect for brown-bagging and up-the-mountain munching. Rather nice spread with sweet butter or cream cheese and topped with lox or your favourite cheese. Excellent toasted, too. You'll need to start this one in the morning as it does require 3 risings.

Mixture 1:

1½	cups boiling water	375 mL
¼	cup vegetable shortening	50 mL
½	cup molasses	125 mL
1	Tbs. dry instant coffee	15 mL
2	tsp. salt	10 mL

Mixture 2:

1	Tbs. active dry yeast	15 mL
½	cup lukewarm water	125 mL
½	tsp. granulated sugar	2 mL

Mixture 3:

2	cups rye flour	500 mL
2	cups wholewheat flour	500 mL
1	Tbs. cocoa powder	15 mL
2	cups all-purpose flour	500 mL

Extras:

1	cup raisins, plumped*	250 mL
2	Tbs. cornmeal	25 mL

1. In large mixing bowl, melt shortening in hot water. Stir in molasses, dry coffee granules, and salt. Cool to room temperature.
2. In small container, sprinkle yeast over lukewarm water with sugar added. Let soften for 10 minutes. Add to above cooled mixture.
3. To the rye and wholewheat flour, add cocoa powder and mix this into the liquid mixture. Beat until smooth. With hands, blend in remaining all-purpose flour (more, if necessary) to make a firm, but pliable dough.

4. Knead at least 10 minutes. Grease ball of dough and return to large bowl. Cover with towel. Let stand in a warm place until double in bulk, 3-4 hours.

5. Punch down dough and knead in raisins. Cover and let rise again.

6. Divide dough into 2 balls and set on large baking sheet sprinkled with cornmeal. Flatten each ball slightly. Cover. Let rise until double in bulk.

7. Preheat oven. Bake for about 50 minutes until nicely browned or until loaves sound hollow when tapped.

* To plump raisins, soak in warm water for 10 minutes. Squeeze gently to remove excess moisture.

HERBED FOCACCIA

Oven: 450F/230C
Bake: 15-20 min.
Serves: 8-10

Facaccia (fo-kah-cha), the dimpled Italian flat bread is really a first cousin to the thick-crusted pizza. It is wonderful served as is, with soup or a salad. It can also be topped with tomato sauce and shredded mozzarella, and if you like salami or coppa. For the best flavour, use a mild virgin olive oil. A good focaccia should have a rippled surface with a chewy, slightly-crisp texture.

1¼	cups lukewarm water	300 mL
½	tsp. granulated sugar	2 mL
1	Tbs. active dry yeast	15 mL
2	Tbs. fruity olive oil	25 mL
½	tsp. salt	2 mL
3	cups all-purpose flour	750 mL
	Topping:	
	Olive oil for brushing	
	Seasoned salt or garlic salt	
2	green onions, chopped	2
1	tsp. dried basil leaves	5 mL
1	tsp. dried oregano leaves	5 mL

1. In a large mixing bowl, combine the water with sugar. Sprinkle yeast over top. Let stand 10 minutes for yeast to soften and bubble up.
2. Stir in olive oil and salt. Then add flour mixing with hands. Turn out onto lightly-floured surface. Knead, adding more flour as necessary to make a soft but firm dough.
3. Grease ball of dough and return to bowl. Cover with towel and let rise in warm place until double in bulk, about 1 hour.
4. Punch down dough. Roll out into large rectangle patting and stretching to fit bottom of large baking sheet that has been well greased with olive oil.
5. With finger, gently press indentations (not holes) all over dough. Brush surface with olive oil and then lightly sprinkle with your favourite seasoned salt, the chopped onions, and herbs. Let stand in a warm place, uncovered for about 30 minutes to rise again.

6. Preheat oven. Bake focaccia for about 15 minutes until golden. Remove to large rack, otherwise bottom will "sweat" and be soggy. Cut into squares and serve warm. Focaccia may be frozen, but cool completely before wrapping. Crispen in warm oven for about 10 minutes.

NOTE: The above dough makes excellent pizzas.

TOMATO SAUCE for PIZZA

Simmer: 20 min.
Makes: 1½ cups/375 mL

A good basic sauce to use for pizza or the above focaccia.

2 Tbs.	good olive oil	25 mL
1 med.	onion, finely chopped	1
1 lrg.	clove garlic, minced	1
1 sm.	tin tomato sauce	213 mL
1 sm.	tin tomato paste	156 mL
2 tsp.	granulated sugar	10 mL
1 tsp.	dried leaf oregano	5 mL
1 tsp.	dried basil leaves	5 mL
½ tsp.	salt	2 mL
½ tsp.	freshly-ground pepper	2 mL

Heat oil in a heavy saucepan and gently saute onion and garlic until tender. Add remaining ingredients with seasonings to taste. Simmer gently for 20-25 minutes. Cool before using.

GARLICKY FRENCH BREAD

Oven: 350F/180C
Bake: 20-25 min.
Serves: 6

1	lrg. loaf French bread, unsliced	1
¾	cup soft butter or margarine	175 mL
1	lrg. clove garlic, finely minced	1
1	Tbs. finely minced parsley (opt.)	15 mL
1	sm. pinch cayenne	1

This one never fails to please the barbecue crowd. May be completely made ahead and frozen. Good with egg twist, too.

1. Slice bread diagonally at 1 in./2.5 cm intervals without cutting through to bottom.
2. Combine remaining ingredients in mixing bowl and cream together. Spread generously between bread slices.
3. Wrap the whole thing in foil. Bake in preheated oven until completely heated through.

PARMESAN-GARLIC HOTSIES

Broil: 2-3 min
Serves: 6-8

1	med. Italian loaf, unsliced	1
¾	cup soft butter or margarine	175 mL
½	cup freshly grated Parmesan	125 mL
¼	cup minced parsley	50 mL
¼	tsp. garlic powder (not salt)	1 mL
¼	tsp. salt	1 mL
1	lrg. pinch cayenne	1

A run-away favourite with spaghetti, lasagne, or barbecued steaks.

1. Cut bread into 1½ in./4 cm slices. In small mixing bowl, combine remaining ingredients, mixing well. Spread evenly over each slice of bread.
2. Place on large baking sheet (may be frozen) and place under preheated broiler until golden and bubbly. Demolish while hot!

ALMOND LACE CURLS

Oven: 350F/180C
Bake: 8 min.
Makes: 12

¼	cup butter or margarine	50 mL
¼	cup granulated sugar	50 mL
1	Tbs. Amaretto or milk	15 mL
¼	cup finely ground almonds	50 mL
1	Tbs. all-purpose flour	15 mL
	Whipped cream (opt.)	

These snappy delights are not difficult to make, but do require a quick, deft hand. The scrolls may be filled with piped-in whipped cream which makes them a very special treat for Christmas or Valentine's Day.

1. Preheat oven. Generously grease and flour a medium-size baking sheet.
2. In medium saucepan, melt the butter with sugar. Remove from heat and add liqueur, mixing well. Stir in almonds and flour until smooth and slightly thickened.
3. Drop by teaspoonful (only 4 at a time and as far apart as possible) onto prepared sheet. Bake about 8 minutes or until lacey and golden-brown.
4. Cool for 1 minute. Then quickly lift up, one at a time with wide spatula. Turn upside down on working surface, and as fast as you can, roll around handle of wooden spoon. If cookies cool too fast and are too brittle, return to oven for 1-2 minutes.
5. Best eaten same day as they are made; otherwise store in airtight container. If using whipped cream, pipe into cylinders just before serving time.

CHOCOLATE CHIP-OATMEAL COLOSSALS

Oven: 375F/190C
Bake: 10-12 min.
Makes: about 15

Always a winner with the younger crowd. Makes a good fund-raiser.

Mixture 1:
2	cups all-purpose flour	500 mL
1	tsp. baking soda	5 mL
½	tsp. salt	2 mL

Mixture 2:
1	cup soft butter or margarine	250 mL
1	cup brown sugar, lightly packed	250 mL
½	cup granulated sugar	125 mL
2	lrg. eggs	2
1	tsp. vanilla	5 mL

Extras:
2	cups regular rolled oats	500 mL
1	cup chocolate chips	250 mL
1	cup raisins or chopped nuts	250 mL

1. Mixture 1: Combine in medium mixing bowl. Set aside.
2. Mixture 2: In larger bowl, cream together the butter with both sugars. Beat in eggs and vanilla until light and fluffy.
3. Add flour mixture to creamed mixture, blending well. Then add the extras (best done with hands).
4. Form balls of a ¼ cup/50 mL dough each. Place on lightly greased baking sheet (four will fit onto large baking sheet just nicely). Flatten each into 5 in./12 cm rounds.
5. Bake in preheated oven for about 10 minutes or until golden. Cool briefly. Remove to racks to cool completely.

CRACKLE-TOPPED GINGERSNAPS

Oven: 350F/180C
Bake: 15 min.
Yields: 3-4 doz.

Crisp and crunchy. Just like the kind Grandma used to make. We especially like these at Christmastime.

2	cups flour (half wholewheat)	500 mL
2	tsp. baking soda	10 mL
1	tsp. ground ginger	5 mL
1	tsp. cinnamon	5 mL
½	tsp. cloves	2 mL
¼	tsp. salt	1 mL
1	cup dark brown sugar	250 mL
¾	cup vegetable shortening	175 mL
1	lrg. egg	1
¼	cup dark molasses	50 mL
	Granulated sugar for dipping	

1. In a medium mixing bowl, combine flour, soda, spices, and salt. Mix well with whisk. Set aside.
2. In a larger bowl, cream together sugar and shortening. Beat in egg and molasses. Add flour mixture, mixing until well-blended.
3. Form 1 in./2.5 cm balls and roll in sugar. Place on greased baking sheet. Flatten slightly with tines of fork. Bake in preheated oven for 10-12 minutes until tops are firm and crackled.

DUTCH SHORTBREAD

Oven: 325F/160C
Bake: 30 min.
Yields: 6-7 doz.

6¼	cups all-purpose flour	1550 mL
½	tsp. baking soda	2 mL
2¼	cups unsalted butter, softened	550 mL
½	cup soft vegetable shortening	125 mL
1¾	cups granulated sugar	425 mL
1	lb. deluxe fruit mix	500 g
½	cup chopped walnuts	125 mL

1. Combine flour and baking soda in plastic bag. Mix and set aside. In a very large bowl (punch bowl), cream together butter and shortening until well blended.
2. Add sugar, beating until light and fluffy. Next add flour mixture. Mix and knead with hands until dough becomes crackly in texture. Blend in the fruit and nuts.
3. Line 15x10 in./2 L rimmed baking sheet with wax paper and then spread dough evenly into it. Chill several hours or freeze until firm.
4. Preheat oven. Turn out slab of dough onto cutting board. Peel off paper. Slice into fingers with very sharp knife.
5. Place on ungreased baking sheet. Prick with fork. Bake until light-golden, about 30 minutes. Cool and then store in airtight container. These freeze well.

We never let the festive season go by without a batch or two of these fabulous tasting cookies. Makes a large quantity, but somehow they never seem to last. From one of my favourite cooks, Janet Kalkman.

MARITIME OATCAKES

Oven: 375F/190C
Bake: 15-20 min.
Yields: 15 lrg.

During my visit to Halifax in the summer of 1982, I took a liking to oatcakes. They seemed to come in all shapes and sizes, but I decided that I liked them best in thin giant rounds. These oatcakes are wonderfully crisp — excellent for nibbling.

1½	cups all-purpose flour	375 mL
1½	cups rolled oats	375 mL
¼	cup brown sugar	50 mL
½	tsp. baking soda	2 mL
½	tsp. salt	2 mL
½	cup vegetable shortening	125 mL
¼	cup chilled butter	50 mL
½	cup cold water	125 mL
	Extra rolled oats for rolling	

1. In large mixing bowl, combine flour, oats, brown sugar, soda, and salt. Cut in shortening and butter with pastry blender or 2 knives until mixture resembles coarse crumbs.

2. Sprinkle in water (more or less) — just enough to hold mixture together. Divide into 15 balls.

3. On surface scattered with oats, roll out each portion very thin. Edges will be jagged, but that's what gives these such a homey touch. With wide spatula, transfer to ungreased baking sheet.

4. Bake in preheated oven for about 15 minutes until crisp and golden. Cool completely before storing. To restore crispiness, rewarm in oven for a few minutes.

APRICOT BARS

Oven: 350F/180C
Bake: 50-55 min.
Yields: 16 bars

This recipe came printed on the back of a package of nuts I once bought. A fantabulous treat for any gathering.

Base:
½	cup butter, softened	125 mL
2	Tbs. brown sugar	25 mL
1	cup all-purpose flour	250 mL

Filling:
¾	cup dried apricots	175 mL
	Boiling water	
1/3	cup all-purpose flour	75 mL
½	tsp. baking powder	2 mL
¼	tsp. salt	1 mL
1	cup packed brown sugar	250 mL
2	lrg. eggs	2
1	tsp. vanilla	5 mL
½	cup chopped walnuts	125 mL

Topping:
Powdered sugar or icing

1. Base: Cream together butter and sugar in medium mixing bowl. Add flour, mixing until crumbly. Press into 8 in./20 cm sq. baking pan. Bake in preheated oven for 20 minutes until golden. Cool.

2. Filling: Place apricots in small saucepan with boiling water to cover. Cook 10 minutes or until tender. Drain, cool, and then chop. Set aside.

3. Combine flour, baking powder, and salt. Mix well and set aside. In a larger bowl, beat together sugar, eggs, and vanilla. Add flour mixture, stirring with wooden spoon to mix. Fold in chopped apricots and nuts. Spread over cooled base.

4. Bake 30 minutes or until golden. Cool. Sprinkle lightly with sifted powdered sugar or spread with tangy lemon icing. Cut into bars.

MATRIMONIAL DATE SQUARES

Oven: 350F/180C
Bake: 50 min.
Yields: 16 bars

These date-laden oatmeal bars or squares are said to have originated in Wales where they were served at tea parties and wedding celebrations. For many-a-young bride settling in Canada, matrimonial cake was almost always included among her repertoire of treasured "receipts".

Crust:

2	cups lrg. flake oats	500 mL
1	cup all-purpose flour	250 mL
½	cup brown sugar	125 mL
½	tsp. baking soda	2 mL
¾	cup butter or margarine	175 mL

Filling:

1½	cups pitted dates, chopped	375 mL
1	cup water	250 mL
2	Tbs. brown sugar	25 mL
½	sm. lemon, for juice	½

1. Preheat oven. In medium mixing bowl, combine oats, flour, brown sugar, and baking soda. Mix well. Add butter and "work in" with fingers until crumbly. Press 2/3 of it into 8 in./2 L sq. pan. Bake 10 minutes. Cool slightly.

2. While crust is baking, combine dates, water, brown sugar, and lemon juice in saucepan. Cook over medium heat until smooth and well blended. Cool and then spread over crust. Sprinkle remaining crumble over top. Bake another 40 minutes until nicely browned. Cool and then cut into bars.

APPLE-MINCE FILLING: Combine 2 cups/500 mL mincemeat, 2 chopped green apples, and 1 Tbs./15 mL sugar. Spread over crust.

MOUNTAIN MOMENTS

Oven: 350F/180C
Bake: 30 min.
Makes: 16 squares

These high-energy treats are excellent for backpacking, picnicking, or brown bagging.

Mixture 1:

½	cup butter or margarine	125 mL
½	cup brown sugar, packed	125 mL
1	lrg. egg	1
1	tsp. vanilla	5 mL

Mixture 2:

1	cup rolled oats	250 mL
½	cup unbleached flour	125 mL
½	tsp. baking powder	2 mL
1	cup chopped walnuts	250 mL
1	cup chocolate chips	250 mL
1	cup dark raisins	250 mL

Topping:

3	Tbs. wheat germ	50 mL

1. Preheat oven. Grease 9 in/23 cm baking pan.
2. Soften butter in large mixing bowl and cream with sugar until light and fluffy. Beat in egg and vanilla until well blended.
3. Mix in oats, flour, and baking powder. Stir well. Add nuts, chocolate chips, and raisins. Press into prepared pan.
4. Sprinkle top with wheat germ. Bake in preheated oven 30 minutes. Cool. Cut into squares or bars.

RHUBARB MERINGUE SQUARES

Oven: 350F/180C
Serves: 6-8

Our good friends, the Dycks live up in the Peace River Country in northern Alberta where the rhubarb grows waist-high. Here's a family favourite sent my way, back in May 1981. We love it!

Crust:
1	cup soft butter or margarine	250 mL
1	Tbs. granulated sugar	15 mL
2	cups all-purpose flour	500 mL

Filling:
1½	cups granulated sugar	375 mL
2	Tbs. cornstarch	25 mL
½	cup milk	125 mL
1	med. orange, rind & juice	1
4	cups thinly sliced rhubarb	1 L
3	lrg. egg yolks, lightly beaten	3
½	tsp. grated nutmeg	2 mL

Topping:
3	lrg. egg whites, room temperature	3
4	Tbs. granulated sugar	60 mL
1	tsp. vanilla	5 mL

1. In a medium mixing bowl, cream together butter and sugar. Add flour, mixing until crumbly. Pack into 12x8 in./3 L pan. Bake in preheated oven for 20 minutes or until golden. Cool slightly.

2. Filling: In a large saucepan, combine sugar, cornstarch, milk, orange rind and juice. Stir in the rhubarb. Cook over medium heat until rhubarb is just tender and mixture turns clear.

3. Add a little of the hot mixture to the yolks and stir it back into the pot to thicken. Stir constantly without letting it boil or overcook. Add nutmeg. Spread over crust.

4. Topping: Beat egg whites until soft peaks form. Add sugar gradually, beating until stiff. Add vanilla. Spread over hot mixture. Bake for 10 minutes or until meringue is golden. Cool. Cut into squares.

CURRANT BUTTER TARTS

Oven: 425F/220C
Bake: 20 min.
Yields: 16-18

A year 'round favourite. I make my own pie pastry and line the regular-size muffin tins with rounds of it. That way, each and everybody gets an ample sampling of the ambrosial mixture.

16-18	tart shells, unbaked	16-18
	Filling:	
½	cup butter, melted	125 mL
¾	cup brown sugar	175 mL
½	cup corn syrup	125 mL
1	Tbs. white vinegar	15 mL
1	tsp. vanilla	5 mL
2	lrg. eggs, room temperature	2
¾	cup currants*	175 mL
½	cup chopped walnuts	125 mL

1. Preheat oven. Keep tart shells chilled while making the filling.
2. Place melted butter in large mixing bowl. Cool. Beat in brown sugar, syrup, vinegar, and vanilla. Add eggs and beat until smooth and well blended. Stir in currants and nuts.
3. Fill tart shells only 2/3 full. Do not fill much more as filling will bubble up and overflow. Bake in preheated oven for about 20 minutes until bubbly and brown. Cool slightly before removing from pan.

* VARIATION: Chopped raisins may be used to replace currants.

RUM BALLS from "CHEF on the RUN"

Mature: 2 wks.
Makes: 9-10 doz.

12	oz. pkg. chocolate chips	340 g
1	cup dairy sour cream	250 mL
½	cup almond paste	125 mL
8	cups vanilla wafers, crushed	2 L
3	cups powdered icing sugar	750 mL
2	cups pecans, finely chopped	500 mL
1½	cups butter, melted	375 mL
1½	cups white rum (I use less)*	375 mL
2/3	cup dry cocoa	150 mL
	Chocolate shot or sprinkles	

1. Melt chocolate chips and combine with sour cream, and almond paste. Cream well and set aside.
2. In a larger bowl, combine crushed wafers and the remaining ingredients, except for chocolate shot. Mix until it holds its shape.
3. Add chocolate-sour cream mixture and knead with hands until blended and soft. Refrigerate until firm enough to form a small ball in palm of hand, yet soft enough to pick up the chocolate shot.
4. Take tablespoons of mixture and form balls. Roll in shot and place on trays lined with waxed paper to harden overnight in refrigerator. Put them into tins and refrigerate. They need 2 weeks to mature.
5. If keeping them for more than 4 weeks, they should be frozen. Take them out of the refrigerator a few hours before serving to soften slightly and to bring out the rum flavour.

* I find that 1 cup/250 mL rum is just right for my taste, but adjust more or less according to your own preference.

These ARE without a doubt, the best rum balls you could ever make! The secret? It's more than the rum. It's the sour cream and the almond paste that add that unique touch to the recipe. Adapted from Diane Clement's "Chef on the Run" (1982).

STRAWBERRIES with RASPBERRY SAUCE

Serves: 4-6

To strawberry aficionados, this may seem like gilding the lily, but the raspberry sauce does add a scintillating sparkle and lively flavour to berries in season.

1	qt. fresh strawberries	1 L
	Sauce:	
1	pkg. frozen raspberries in syrup	425 g
⅓	cup red currant jelly (not jam)	75 mL
1	Tbs. cornstarch	15 mL
1	Tbs. fresh lemon juice	15 mL
	Garnish:	
	Whipped cream, Mint sprigs	

1. Hull and quickly rinse strawberries. Pat dry. Halve, if large. Chill until serving time.

2. Thaw and drain raspberries in sieve over saucepan. You should have close to 1 cup/250 mL syrup. To the liquid, add currant jelly and cornstarch. Stir to blend in starch.

3. Place mixture over medium heat, stirring constantly until bubbly and slightly thickened. Remove from heat and add lemon juice. Cool and chill.

4. At serving time, spoon sauce over individual servings of berries. If desired, garnish each with a swirl of whipped cream and a mint sprig.

NOTE: Any leftover sauce is delicious over vanilla ice-cream or other fresh fruit.

MELON in RUM-LIME SAUCE

Chill: 4 hrs.

Perfect for late-summer entertaining. From my friend, Margaret Kruger, who had a "big hand" in exposing me to the wonderful world of food and cooking.

	Syrup:	
2/3	cup granulated sugar	150 mL
1/3	cup water	75 mL
1	tsp. grated lime rind	5 mL
1/2	cup light rum	125 mL
6	Tbs. fresh lime juice	90 mL
	Fruit:	
1	med. cantaloupe	1
1	med. honeydew melon	1
1/4	sm. watermelon	1/4
1	cup fresh blueberries	250 mL

1. Syrup: Combine sugar, and water in a small saucepan. Bring to a boil. Reduce heat and let simmer 5 minutes. Remove from heat and add rind. Cool to room temperature. Add rum and lime juice. May be done the day before.
2. Seed melons. Using a melon baller, cut cantaloupe, honeydew, and watermelon into balls. Place in your prettiest glass bowl along with blueberries. Pour cooled syrup over. Chill 4-6 hours.

LEMON LUSH

Serves: 4

3	cups fresh raspberries, blueberries, or blackberries	750 mL
	Curd:	
⅓	cup unsalted butter	75 mL
¾	cup granulated sugar	175 mL
2	tsp. grated lemon rind	10 mL
½	cup fresh lemon juice	125 mL
3	lrg. eggs, room temperature	3

1. Quickly rinse berries. Drain and pat very dry. Keep chilled until ready to use.
2. Curd: Melt butter in top of double boiler or a large stainless bowl (one that will sit comfortably over smaller pan of hot water). Cool butter slightly.
3. Add remaining curd ingredients, whisking until well blended. Set over gentle simmering water (water should not touch pan) and cook, beating until mixture is thick and smooth, 15-20 minutes. Do not let boil.
4. Cool to room temperature. Alternately layer berries with lemon curd into stemmed glasses. There should be more berries than curd. Chill.

HINT: Before starting, set the eggs and lemons in a mixing bowl with warm water. That way, the eggs will be at the proper temperature and the lemons will yield more juice.

The lemon mixture, really a lemon curd recipe is from family friend, Winnie Brubaker of Calgary. I've carried things a step further by bringing our local berries into the picture. Winnie's lemon curd can be made days, even months ahead; but keep it refrigerated. Nice spread over toast or spooned into baked tiny tart shells with dabs of whipped cream to top.

LEMON ICE in HONEYDEW

Serves: 4

Nice and tangy, particularly after a rich meal. The ice may be served as is, or over fresh fruit and berries in season.

2	sm. honeydew melons	2
	Ice:	
½	cup granulated sugar	125 mL
1	cup cold water	250 mL
2	lrg. lemons, rind & juice	2
	Mint sprigs for garnish	

1. Prepare ice first. Combine sugar and water in a stainless saucepan. Bring to a boil and let simmer 10 minutes to make a light syrup. Cool.

2. Add grated rind and juice (⅓ cup/75 mL-½ cup/125 mL) depending on how tart you like it. Transfer to stainless bowl and freeze until ice forms around edges, about 1½ hours.

3. Beat mixture with fork until smooth. Re-freeze and beat again. Repeat once more to give it a finer texture. Cover tightly and store in freezer until ready to use.

4. To serve, halve honeydew melons and seed. Scoop or mound ice into each cavity and top with mint sprig. If ice is very hard, let stand at room temperature for about 10 minutes to make scooping easier.

SPICY WINE ORANGES

Chill: 6 hrs.
Serves: 4

A refreshing finish to just about any meal!

6	lrg. juicy oranges	6
1	cup water	250 mL
2/3	cup granulated sugar	150 mL
1	cup red wine	250 mL
2	sm. cinnamon sticks	2
4	whole cloves	4
4	slices lemon	4
	Whipped cream for topping	

1. With sharp knife, peel oranges. Slice crosswise and place in a glass bowl.

2. In a medium saucepan, combine water and sugar. Bring to a boil. Lower heat; add wine, spices, and lemon slices. Let simmer gently for 15 minutes. Do not let boil. Cool slightly.

3. Strain still-warm syrup over orange slices. Chill for at least 6 hours before serving. Top each serving with swirl of whipped cream, just barely sweetened.

FABULOUS CHEESECAKE

Oven: 325F/160C
Bake: 55-60 min.
Serves: 8-10

A classic recipe. Serve with fresh berries or a fruit sauce. Must be made ahead.

Crust:
1½	cups crushed graham wafers (25)	375 mL
⅓	cup butter, melted	75 mL

Filling:
3	lrg. pkg. cream cheese	EA.	250 g
1	cup granulated sugar		250 mL
4	lrg. eggs, room temperature		4
1	tsp. vanilla		5 mL

Topping:
1½	cups dairy sour cream	375 mL
2	Tbs. granulated sugar	25 mL
1	tsp. vanilla	5 mL

1. Preheat oven. For crust, combine crushed wafers with melted butter. Mix well and press onto bottom and up sides of 9 in./23 cm springform pan. Bake 10 minutes. Cool.

2. Filling: In a large mixing bowl, beat together softened cream cheese and sugar until smooth. Add eggs, one at a time beating thoroughly after each addition. Stir in vanilla.

3. Pour mixture into cooled crust and bake about 50 minutes or until JUST set. Do not overbake. Remove from oven and let stand for 10 minutes.

4. Meanwhile, combine sour cream, sugar, and vanilla for topping. Spread evenly over hot cheesecake and return to oven for 5 minutes.

5. Cool cheesecake and then chill overnight. Loosen edges of cake with sharp knife and release from pan. Cut into wedges and spoon fresh fruit and juices over top.

PAVLOVA

Oven: 350F/180C
Bake: 1 hr. 15 min.
Serves: 6-8

An institution from "Down Under" created in honour of the visiting ballerina, Anna Pavlova when she toured Australia and New Zealand back in 1926. Ever since, it's been a toss-up as to which country invented the meringue like cake. Pavlova is traditionally topped off with whipped cream and slices of kiwifruit. Truly divine!

4	lrg. eggs, room temperature	4
	Pinch salt	
1	cup fine berry sugar	250 mL
2	tsp. cornstarch	10 mL
1	tsp. white vinegar	5 mL
1	tsp. vanilla	5 mL
	Topping:	
1½	cups heavy cream	375 mL
	Kiwifruit, strawberries	

1. Preheat oven. In a large, grease-free bowl, beat the egg whites with a pinch of salt until high, soft peaks form.
2. Save back 1 Tbs./15 mL of the sugar. Add the remainder, a tablespoon at a time, beating well after each addition until the sugar is dissolved (important!). Mixture should be smooth, stiff, and very glossy.
3. To the reserved sugar, add the cornstarch. Mix well and sprinkle evenly over meringue. Add vinegar and vanilla. With large spoon, lightly but thoroughly fold together. Do not beat or overmix!
4. Mound (I like to use a piping bag with a large star tip) into 7 in./18 cm circle onto baking sheet lined with heavy foil. Flatten top slightly.
5. Reduce heat to 275F/140C and immediately place pavlova inside. Bake, without disturbing for 1 hr. 15 minutes until light beige in colour. Turn off oven and allow cake to cool completely. May be made the day before, but wrap in foil and store in a cool, dry place.

6. Shortly before serving, carefully peel off the foil from pavlova and place on serving platter. Whip cream (do not sweeten) and spread over cake. Garnish top with sliced kiwifruit and halved berries. Serve in wedges.

NOTE: To ensure that your egg whites will beat up to a good consistency and volume, use eggs that are a few days old. Fresh whites are too thin. The whites must also be at room temperature and beaten up in a very clean, grease-free bowl.

STRAWBERRY MERINGUE TORTE

Oven: 350F/180C
Bake: 40 min.
Serves: 6-8

High school teacher and avid sportsman, David Wei gave me this real gem of a recipe. It's a double-decker treat laden with Grand Marnier-tinged whipped cream and strawberries in season.

Cake:
1	cup lightly-spooned cake flour	250 mL
2½	tsp. baking powder	12 mL
¼	tsp. salt	1 mL
½	cup soft shortening or butter	125 mL
½	cup granulated sugar	125 mL
4	lrg. egg yolks	4
1	tsp. vanilla	5 mL
⅓	cup milk	75 mL

Meringue:
4	lrg. egg whites, room temperature	4
1	cup granulated sugar	250 mL
1	tsp. vanilla	5 mL

Filling:
2	cups heavy cream	500 mL
2	Tbs. powdered icing sugar	25 mL
1	Tbs. Grand Marnier liqueur	15 mL

Topping:
1	qt. fresh strawberries, hulled	1 L
¼	cup Grand Marnier liqueur	50 mL
2	Tbs. granulated sugar	25 mL

1. Preheat oven. Grease and line 2-9 in./23 cm round cake pans with wax paper.

2. Sift together cake flour, baking powder, and salt. Set aside. In a large mixing bowl, cream shortening or butter with sugar until light and fluffy. Beat in yolks and vanilla. Mix well.

3. Add sifted flour mixture and the milk in alternate thirds, mixing just until smooth. Spoon HALF of the batter into each of the prepared pans.

4. Meringue: In a large grease-free bowl, beat egg whites until soft peaks form. Gradually (important!), beat in the sugar until stiff meringue forms. Fold in vanilla.

5. Top batter with meringue, spreading it right to the very edges of pans. Bake in preheated oven until meringue is brown and crisp. Cool before removing wax paper.

6. Just before serving time, whip cream (for filling) until thickened. Add icing sugar and liqueur to taste. Slather HALF of the whipped cream between cake layers and the remainder on top.

7. Topping: Slice berries and sweeten with liqueur and sugar. Spoon over cake and serve immediately.

HONEY of A CARROT CAKE

Oven: 350F/180C
Bake: as directed
Serves: 10-12

Honey makes this cake extra moist. It's also brimming with other good things — like carrots, raisins, and nuts.

Mixture 1:

2½	cups all-purpose flour	625 mL
2	tsp. baking powder	10 mL
1	tsp. baking soda	5 mL
2	tsp. cinnamon	10 mL
½	tsp. nutmeg	2 mL
½	tsp. ground ginger	2 mL
½	tsp. salt	2 mL

Mixture 2:

3	cups finely shredded carrots	750 mL
1	cup golden raisins	250 mL
½	cup chopped walnuts	125 mL
½	cup medium-fine cocoanut	125 mL

Mixture 3:

4	lrg. eggs, room temperature	4
½	cup brown sugar	125 mL
1	cup liquid honey	250 mL
1	cup salad oil	250 mL

1. Preheat oven. Grease large tube pan with removable bottom or a 9x5 in./3 L baking pan.
2. In a medium bowl, combine dry ingredients (Mixture 1). Mix well with whisk and set aside. In another bowl, combine carrots, raisins, nuts, and cocoanut. Also set aside.
3. In a large mixing bowl, beat eggs with sugar until well blended. Slowly dribble in honey, beating all the while. Slowly add the oil, beating thoroughly.
4. To the creamy mixture, add the flour mixture, stirring with wooden spoon just until moistened. Gently fold in the carrot mixture. Do not beat or overmix.

5. Pour batter into prepared pan. Bake in preheated oven about 1 hour 10 minutes in tube pan OR 50 minutes in shallow baking dish. Test for doneness with skewer. Cool.

6. Ice or frost as desired. Delicious with orange butter icing or cream cheese frosting.

CARROT APPLE CAKE: Finely grate carrots to measure 1½ cups/375 mL and coarsely-grated apples to measure the same (both lightly packed).

FROSTINGS for CARROT CAKE

ORANGE BUTTER ICING: Combine 2½ cups/625 mL icing sugar, 2 Tbs./25 mL soft butter or margarine, and the grated rind and juice of 1 lrg. orange. Beat well to blend. Spread over top of cooled cake.

CREAM CHEESE FROSTING: Cream together 8 oz./250 g soft cream cheese and ½ cup/125 mL soft butter or margarine. Add 2 cups/500 mL powdered icing sugar, 1 tsp.5 mL vanilla, and a little milk or lemon juice. Beat until velvety smooth.

THE DEFINITIVE CHOCOLATE CAKE

Oven: 350F/180C
Bake: 25 min.
Serves: 8-10

For a long time, this was the Lazy Gourmet's guarded secret. This satanic delight is just one of the 92 indulgences revealed in "Nuts About Chocolate" by Vancouver caterers, Susan Mendelson and Deborah Roitberg.

Mixture 1:
2¼	cups all-purpose flour	550 mL
1½	tsp. baking soda	7 mL
1½	tsp. baking powder	7 mL

Mixture 2:
2	lrg. eggs, room temperature	2
1	cup granulated sugar	250 mL
2	Tbs. soft butter	25 mL
1	cup vegetable oil	250 mL
½	cup dry cocoa, packed	125 mL
½	cup buttermilk	125 mL
1	tsp. vanilla	5 mL

Mixture 3:
1	cup boiling water	250 mL
½	cup chocolate chips	125 mL

1. Preheat oven. Grease two 8 in./20 cm-9 in./23 cm round cake pans and line with waxed paper.
2. Combine flour, baking soda, and baking powder. Set aside. Using a large mixing bowl, beat ingredients in Mixture 2, adding each in the order listed.
3. Add flour mixture, stirring with wooden spoon just until blended. Fold in boiling water until smooth. Divide mixture into prepared pans. Sprinkle with chocolate chips.

4. Bake in preheated oven for about 25 minutes or until toothpick inserted in centre comes out clean. Cool. Spread layers with the Lazy Gourmet's Incredible Chocolate Icing.

INCREDIBLE CHOCOLATE ICING

You can combine these ingredients with an electric mixer, but the texture will not be the same. A Lazy Gourmet recipe.

1½	cups powdered icing sugar	375 mL
1	cup dry cocoa	250 mL
¾	cup soft butter	175 mL
3	Tbs. hot coffee	50 mL
3	Tbs. milk	50 mL
1½	tsp. vanilla	7 mL

Place icing sugar, cocoa, and soft butter in processor fitted with steel blade. Blend for 4 seconds. Add hot coffee, milk, and vanilla, blending until smooth. Additional milk will make a thinner icing.

ROMY'S CHOCOLATE DREAM

Oven: 350F/180C
Bake: 30 min.
Serves: 8-10

Cooking instructor, Romy Reimann is a whiz with the processor. In fact, she was the one who introduced me to the wonders of this machine. A rave recipe for those who crave a little "black magic".

6	lrg. eggs, separated	6
5½	oz. semi-sweet chocolate	150 g
1½	cups pecans or walnuts	375 mL
2	Tbs. all-purpose flour	25 mL
¾	cup butter, softened	175 mL
¾	cup granulated sugar	175 mL
	Chocolate Mousse (follows)	

1. Preheat oven. Butter and lightly flour a 10 in./25.5 cm springform pan. Separate eggs and let stand at room temperature.
2. Chop chocolate into small pieces and melt over gentle simmering water. Cool to room temperature.
3. Place nuts and flour in processor bowl with steel blade. Process until fine. Set aside.
4. In large mixing bowl, cream together the butter and sugar until light and fluffy. Add yolks, one at a time beating thoroughly.
5. In a separate bowl using clean beaters, beat egg whites until firm peaks form. Set aside.
6. Add melted chocolate and nut mixture to the butter-egg mixture. Then fold in the beaten whites, a small portion at first to lighten the batter (best done with whisk). Do not beat, but do mix thoroughly.
7. Pour batter into prepared pan. Bake until cake is "springy" to the touch and tester comes out clean. Cool completely.
8. While cake is still in pan, top with mousse and then freeze, for at least 2 hours to firm. If desired, decorate with pecan halves, candied violets, or shaved chocolate. Loosen cake from pan and serve in wedges.

MOUSSE for CHOCOLATE DREAM

3½	oz. semi-sweet chocolate	100 g
¼	cup hot water	50 mL
1	Tbs. instant coffee granules	15 mL
¼	cup granulated sugar	50 mL
2	lrg. egg yolks	2
1	cup heavy cream, whipped	250 mL

1. Chop chocolate into small pieces and place in work bowl of processor mounted with steel blade. Process into fine bits. Set aside.

2. In a heavy saucepan, combine hot water, instant coffee, and sugar. Cook over moderate heat, adding chocolate until melted. Cool about 5 minutes, stirring occasionally.

3. Add yolks, one at a time beating well after each addition. Cool and then chill. Fold whipped cream into chocolate mixture.

PURPLE PLUM TORTE

Oven: 375F/190C
Bake: 50 min.
Serves: 6

September means plum time. Here's one delicious way of dealing with the fruit. Best served warm with a swirl of whipped cream or a spoonful of good vanilla ice-cream.

18-20	ripe Italian plums	18-20
	Batter:	
1	cup all-purpose flour	250 mL
1	tsp. baking powder	5 mL
¼	tsp. salt	1 mL
1	cup granulated sugar	250 mL
½	cup soft butter	125 mL
2	lrg. eggs, room temperature	2
½	cup milk	125 mL
	Topping:	
2	Tbs. granulated sugar	25 mL
1	tsp. cinnamon	5 mL

1. Preheat oven. Grease a 9 in./23 cm springform pan. Halve and pit plums. Set aside.
2. Batter: Combine flour, baking powder, and salt in a medium mixing bowl. In a larger one, beat together sugar and butter until creamy smooth. Add eggs, one at a time, beating well after each addition.
3. Add dry mixture, alternating with milk. Stir with large spoon ONLY until blended. Do not beat or overmix. Spread into prepared pan.
4. Cover top with halved plums (cut-side down), pushing them down into batter.
5. Combine topping of sugar and cinnamon. Sprinkle over plums. Bake about 50 minutes or until golden and centre is baked through (test with toothpick). Serve warm.

PEACH of A PIE

Chill: 6 hrs.
Serves: 6-8

After you've tried this one, you'll wonder how anything so good, could possibly take so little time to make. A treasured family favourite from Esther Reid of Penticton.

9	in. pastry shell, baked	23 cm
6	med. peaches, ripened	6
1	cup granulated sugar	250 mL
½	cup water	125 mL
4	Tbs. cornstarch	60 mL
1	med. lemon, for juice	1
	Whipped cream for topping	

1. Cool pastry shell and set aside.
2. Skin and thinly slice ONLY 2 peaches. Place over heat in medium saucepan with sugar and water. Mash fruit until finely pureed (I do this in the blender). Add and bring to a boil.
3. In a small container, combine cornstarch, lemon juice, and if needed, a little water. Add this paste to peach mixture, stirring constantly over medium heat until bubbly and thickened, about 3 minutes. Cool.
4. Skin and thinly slice the remaining peaches. Add to cooked mixture. Pour into pie shell. Cool and then chill for at least 6 hours or until set.
5. Before serving, whisk cream until thick. Flavour with just a little sugar and vanilla. Spread over pie. Best served the day it's made.

HINT: To skin peaches, dip into boiling water until skins slip easily, about 1 minute. Quickly dip into cold water. Peel.

"EASY AS PIE" PASTRY

Makes: 4 single shells or 2 double-crusted pies

2½	cups all-purpose flour	625 mL
½	tsp. baking powder	2 mL
½	tsp. salt	2 mL
1	cup firm lard	250 mL
1	med. egg yolk	1
1½	tsp. regular vinegar	7 mL
	Cold water	

1. In a large mixing bowl, combine flour, baking powder and salt. Add lard and cut in, using a pastry blender or two knives. Mixture should resemble coarse crumbs.

2. In a large measuring cup, combine egg yolk and vinegar. Mix in enough water to measure ½ cup/125 mL liquid in total. Add to flour mixture and toss gently, but quickly to moisten.

3. If mixture feels dry and will not gather into a soft (not sticky) ball, then run your hand under cold water tap and sprinkle in extra liquid. Handle as little as possible.

4. Form 4 balls, slightly flattened. Wrap tightly to chill, at least 1 hour. May be stored for a longer time by freezing (up to 3 months).

TO ROLL OUT PASTRY: Let dough soften slightly at room temperature. Flour surface and gently roll out flattened round of dough, always from centre toward edges and keeping a round shape. Fit into pan without stretching. Trim and flute. Then re-use leftover pieces.

A recipe I like. Never fails and turns out so flaky and tender. It's all in the lard and a quick, light hand during the mixing. After a few times, you will develop a "feel" and know exactly when and how much liquid to add.

BAKED SINGLE CRUST:
- Using scissors, trim edge of pastry leaving a 1 in./2.5 cm overhang. Turn overhang under to form a narrow rolled rim. Crimp or flute.
- Prick crust all over with fork. Do this lightly without leaving large holes. Line with piece of foil, one that can be lifted out easily and fill with dried peas or beans (save to use over).
- Bake in preheated 400F/200C oven for 10 minutes. Remove and carefully lift up foil with peas or beans.
- Return to oven to bake an extra few minutes depending on whether pastry is to be partially or fully baked.
- A partially-baked crust will require about 5 minutes extra baking time; a fully-baked one, about 10 minutes or until it is golden-brown. Lightly prick any large bubbles that appear throughout the baking.

EASY GRAHAM CRUST

Oven: 375F/190C
Makes: 1 crust

Especially good with cream-based pies.

⅓	cup butter or margarine	75 mL
1¼	cups graham wafer crumbs	300 mL
½	tsp. cinnamon (opt.)	2 mL

Melt butter or margarine in a small saucepan. Add graham wafer crumbs and if you wish cinnamon. Press into 9 in./23 cm pie plate. Bake in preheated oven for 6-8 minutes until slightly browned. Cool completely before filling.

NOTE: May also be made without baking, but then the crust does not have a nice, crisp texture to it. Simply freeze it for 1 hour. Then fill.

MACADAMIA NUT CREAM PIE

Serves: 6

The macadamia nut tree is actually native to the tropical forests of New South Wales and Queensland in Australia, but has adapted extremely well to Hawaiian soil. Honokaa on the Big Island is now the largest exporter of this rare and noble nut. A "rave" from the Hilton in Hawaii.

Crust:
9	in. baked pie shell (Pastry or graham wafer)	23 cm

Custard:
½	cup granulated sugar	125 mL
4	Tbs. cornstarch	60 mL
¼	tsp. salt	1 mL
2	cups milk	500 mL
3	lrg. egg yolks, beaten	3
1	Tbs. butter or margarine	15 mL
1	cup heavy cream	250 mL
2	Tbs. Kahlua liqueur*	25 mL
½	cup chopped unsalted macadamias	125 mL

Garnish:
Whole roasted macadamias (6)

1. Make pie crust ahead. Cool completely.
2. In heavy saucepan, combine sugar, cornstarch, and salt. Add milk, blending well. Place over medium heat, stirring constantly until smooth and thickened, about 10 minutes.
3. Mix a little of the hot filling into beaten egg yolks and then return to pan. Cook and stir for an additional 3 minutes. Do not let boil, otherwise custard will curdle.
4. Remove from heat. Stir in butter until melted. Cool over pan of cold water, stirring often for the first 10 minutes so that "skin" does not form on top.
5. When custard is completely cooled, whip cream until stiff. Add ONLY ½ cup/125 mL whipped cream, flavouring, and all, but 1 Tbs./15 mL chopped macadamias to cooled custard.

6. Fill pie shell with mixture. Sprinkle with reserved chopped nuts. Then spread remaining whipped cream on top. Chill at least 6 hours or overnight. Just before serving, garnish each wedge with a whole macadamia nut.

* Kahlua may be replaced with 1 tsp./5 mL vanilla.

FAVOURITE RICE PUDDING

**Simmer: 50 min.
Serves: 4**

1	qt. milk	1 L
½	cup raw rice	125 mL
¼	cup granulated sugar	50 mL
½	cup dark raisins	125 mL
¼	tsp. nutmeg	1 mL
1	tsp. vanilla	5 mL

1. In large, heavy saucepan (a must), slowly bring the milk to a boil. Do not let it scorch. Add rice and sugar, stirring until mixture is heated up again. Cover and let simmer gently on very low heat for 20 minutes. Do not disturb.
2. Uncover. Mixture will be liquidy. Add raisins and nutmeg. Cook, stirring often until thickened like custard, about 30 minutes. Flavour with vanilla. Let cool slightly.
3. Pour into large serving bowl or individual dessert dishes. Delicious warm or chilled. For that extra-special touch, serve with a swirl of whipped cream and a sprinkling of toasted sliced almonds.

A frequently requested dessert that's brimming with flavour and goodness. Easy on the budget and calories, too. Make it when you feel "down" and crave for a little warmth and comfort.

DOWN-HOME RHUBARB CRUMBLE

Oven: 350F/180C
Bake: 45-55 min.
Serves: 4-6

A springtime treat with an old-fashioned flavour. Serve with a dollop of whipped cream or vanilla ice-cream.

6	cups sliced rhubarb	1.5 L
2	tsp. grated orange rind	10 mL
½	cup fresh orange juice	125 mL
⅔	cup granulated sugar	150 mL
2	Tbs. all-purpose flour	25 mL
½	tsp. ground nutmeg	2 mL
Topping:		
1	cup all-purpose flour	250 mL
½	cup regular rolled oats	125 mL
½	cup brown sugar, packed	125 mL
½	tsp. baking soda	2 mL
½	cup butter or margarine	125 mL

1. Place unpeeled rhubarb in a large stainless saucepan. Combine with orange rind and juice, granulated sugar, flour, and nutmeg. Mix well.
2. Cook, stirring over medium heat for 5 minutes until sauce is smooth and slightly thickened. Transfer to 9 in./2.5 L glass baking dish or casserole.
3. In a medium mixing bowl, combine flour, oats, brown sugar, and soda. Add butter, mixing with hands until mixture is crumbly. Spread over top of rhubarb mixture.
4. Bake in preheated oven for about 45 minutes or until rhubarb is tender and crumble is golden-brown. Serve warm.

BREAD PUDDING with WHISKEY SAUCE

Oven: 350F/180C
Bake: 45 min.
Serves: 4-6

A simple and unpretentious pudding that is at its best using day-old French or Italian bread. Fabulous touched up with a light drizzle of whiskey sauce.

2	cups cubed day-old bread	500 mL
1	qt. milk	1 L
½	cup granulated sugar	125 mL
2	Tbs. butter or margarine	25 mL
4	lrg. eggs, room temperature	4
1	cup dark raisins	250 mL
1	tsp. vanilla extract	5 mL
½	tsp. nutmeg	2 mL

1. Lightly grease 1½ qt./1.5 L baking dish or casserole. Preheat oven and in it, place a large pan of hot water for pudding dish to "sit in".
2. Cut bread (with crusts on) into 1 in./2.5 cm cubes. Set aside. In large heavy saucepan, heat milk just until tiny bubbles form around edges. Do not let it scorch. Remove from heat.
3. To hot milk, add sugar and butter; then the bread cubes. Let stand 5 minutes. Meanwhile, lightly beat eggs in large mixing bowl. Slowly pour hot mixture over eggs, stirring constantly and gently to mix. Do not break up bread cubes.
4. Add raisins and vanilla. Pour into prepared dish. Sprinkle with nutmeg. Place in hot water bath. Bake in preheated oven until custard is set. Knife inserted in centre should come out clean. Serve warm or chilled with whiskey sauce.

WHISKEY SAUCE: In a large, heavy saucepan (important), combine 1 cup/250 mL EA. of packed brown sugar and heavy cream. Add 3 Tbs./50 mL butter and bring the mixture to a boil. Cook for 2 minutes. Remove from heat and add ⅓ cup/75 mL - ½ cup/125 mL whiskey (to taste). May be made ahead and rewarmed. Serve hot.

RECIPE INDEX

APPETIZERS
Dips and Dunks
   Cool as a Cucumber Dip, 8
   Guacamole (Avocado) Dip, 11
   Layered Nacho Dip, 9
   Mayonnaise for Dip, 21
   Roasted Pepper Cream Cheese, 19
   Salsa Mexicana, 25
   Sassy Eggplant Dip, 20
   Zippy Clam Dunk, 24
Pates and Spreads
   Jalapeno Jelly, 28
   Liver and Mushroom Pate, 13
   Red Salmon Pate, 18
   Terrine of Pork and Veal, 26
Hors d'Oeuvres
   Antipasto, 10
   Cherry Tomato Appetizers, 18
   Gravad Lax (Cured Salmon), 22
   Lemon Tomato Sausage Bites, 23
   Salmon Bellies, 12
   Pickled Mushrooms, 14
   Pismo Beach Clam Tidbits, 15
   Pub-Style Pickled Eggs, 16
   Red Onion-Parsley Rounds, 17

BEEF
   Beef and Potato Combo, 135
   Burritos, 112
   Carbonnade of Beef, 134
   Chimichangas, 110
   Cornish Pasties, 98
   Gringo Chili, 114
   Hungarian Pepper Steak, 133
   Liberal Lasagne, 104
   Roast Brisket of Beef, 132

BREADS
Muffins and Scones
   Blueberry Streusel Muffins, 154
   Chunky Date Bran Muffins, 155
   Island Banana Muffins, 156
   Raisin Buttermilk Scrumpets, 158
   Welsh Cake (Scones), 159
Pancakes
   Spectacular Apple Pancake, 152
   Sunday Morning Pancakes, 150
   Swedish Oatmeal Pancakes, 151
Breads
   Croutons, 75
   Garlicky French Bread, 166
   Herbed Foccacia, 164
   Parmesan Garlic Hotsies, 166
   Pebble Top Soda Bread, 157
   Pizza in a Jiffy, 101
   Raisin Pumpernickel Rounds, 162
   Sticky Cinnamon Buns, 160

BREAKFAST and BRUNCH
   Farmhouse Breakfast, 92
   Golden Crisp Bacon, 92
   Muffins, Pancakes (see BREADS)
   Overnight Brunch, 93
   Poor Man's Omelette, 109

CHICKEN (see POULTRY)

COOKIES, SQUARES, SWEETS
Cookies
    Almond Lace Curls, 168
    Chocolate Oatmeal Colossals, 169
    Crackle-Topped Gingersnaps, 170
    Dutch Shortbread, 171
    Maritime Oatcakes, 172
Squares and Bars
    Apricot Bars, 173
    Matrimonial Date Squares, 174
    Mountain Moments, 175
    Rhubarb Meringue Squares, 176
Sweets
    Rum Balls — Chef on the Run, 178
Tarts
    Currant Butter Tarts, 177
    Lemon Curd for Tarts, 182

DESSERTS
Cakes and Tortes
    Carrot Apple Cake, 190
    Definitive Chocolate Cake, 192
    Fabulous Cheesecake, 185
    Honey of a Carrot Cake, 190
    Pavlova, 186
    Purple Plum Torte, 196
    Romy's Chocolate Dream, 194
    Strawberry Meringue Torte, 188
Berries and Fruit
    Lemon Lush, 182
    Lemon Ice in Honeydew, 183
    Melon in Rum-Lime Sauce, 181
    Spicy Wine Oranges, 184
    Strawberries with Raspberry Sauce, 180
Pies and Pastries
    Easy as Pie Pastry, 198
    Easy Graham Crust, 199
    Macadamia Nut Cream Pie, 200
    Peach of a Pie, 197
    Tarts (see COOKIES)
Puddings and Crumble
    Bread Pudding with Whiskey Sauce, 203
    Down Home Rhubarb Crumble, 202
    Favourite Rice Pudding, 201

FISH and SEAFOOD
Appetizers
    Gravad Lax (Cured Salmon), 22
    Salmon Bellies, 12
    Red Salmon Pate, 18
    Zippy Clam Dunk, 24
Main Entrees
    Deep Cove Fish Patties, 116
    F.O.B. Salmon with Tomato Stuffing, 123
    Golden Sauteed Fish, 126
    Hot Seafood Salad, 120
    Ocean Garden Pasta, 103
    Pan-Fried Trout, 121
    Pasta with Herbed Clam Sauce, 102
    Salmon Kedgeree, 94
    Salmon Teriyaki, 118
    Scalloped Oysters, 119
    Seafood Strudel, 124
    Shrimp in Lemon Garlic Butter, 122
    Tuna Stuffed Bunwiches, 95
    Wei's Salmon Barbecue Sauce, 117
Soups
    Ace-in-the-Hole Clam Chowder, 76
    Corn Oyster Soup, 71
    Garden Halibut Soup, 68

LAMB
Excellent Leg of Lamb, 127
Loin of Lamb Montenegro, 130
Parmesan Coated Lamb Chops, 131
Souvlaki, Tavern-Style, 128

MARINADES (also SAUCES)

MEALS-in-ONE
Burritos, 112
Cacciatore on the Slopes, 106
Caribbean Curried Chicken, 107
Chimichangas, 110
Cornish Pasties, 98
Creole Jambalaya, 108
Farmhouse Breakfast, 92
Golden-Fried Mozzarella, 100
Gringo Chili, 114
Liberal Lasagne, 104
Macaroni and Cheese, 88
Ocean Garden Pasta, 103
Overnight Brunch, 93
Pasta with Clam Sauce, 102
Pizza in a Jiffy, 101
Poor Man's Omelette, 109
Refried Beans, 111
Salmon Kedgeree, 94
Toad-in-the-Hole, 96
Tourtiere, 97
Tuna Stuffed Bunwiches, 95

MEATS (see BEEF, PORK, LAMB)

MUFFINS and PANCAKES (see BREADS)

PASTA and PESTO
Fettuccine and Green Cabbage, 89
Herbed Lemon Orzo, 86
Liberal Lasagne, 104
Macaroni and Cheese, 88
Macaroni Salad, 46
Ocean Garden Pasta, 103
Parsley Pesto for Pasta, 80
Pasta with Herbed Clam Sauce, 102
Pesto with Fresh Basil, 81
Spaetzle with Spinach and Onion, 90

PICKLES and JAMS
Carrot Marmalade, 66
Jalapeno Pepper Jelly, 28
Lemon Curd (Lush), 182
Pickled Beets, 64
Pickled Eggs, Pub-Style, 16
Pickled Mushrooms, 14

PIES and PASTRIES
Crusts
  Easy as Pie Pastry, 198
  Easy Graham Crust, 199
Dessert
  Currant Butter Tarts, 177
  Macadamia Nut Cream Pie, 200
  Peach of a Pie, 197
Meat and Seafood Pies
  Cornish Pasties, 98
  Seafood Strudel, 124
  Tourtiere, 97

PORK, HAM, SAUSAGES
Baked Stuffed Ribs, 137
Burritos, 112
Creole Jambalaya, 108
Farmhouse Breakfast, 92
Frikadeller (Danish Patties), 136
Golden-Crisp Bacon, 92
Indonesian-Style Sate, 138
Lemon-Honey Spareribs, 139
Overnight Brunch, 93
Savory Ham Loaf, 140
Souvlaki, 128
Terrine of Pork and Veal, 26
Toad-in-the-Hole, 96
Tourtiere, 97

POULTRY
Chicken
  Barbecued Ginger Chicken, 142
  Cacciatore on the Slopes, 106
  Caribbean Curried Chicken, 107
  Chicken with Sun-Dried Tomatoes, 143
  Creole Jambalaya, 108
  Honey-Garlic Baked Chicken, 144
  Liver-Mushroom Pate, 13
  Mahogany Wings, 141
  Simply Super Roast Chicken, 145
Duck
  Duck with Blueberries "Richmond", 146
Goose
  Golden Roast Goose, 147
Turkey
  Turkey in the Stew, 148

RICE DISHES also BARLEY, BEANS
Barley Mushroom Pilaf, 87
Fried Rice, Bountiful, 83
Jambalaya Creole, 108
Refried Beans, 111
Rice, Easy Steamed, 82
Rice Pilav with Currants, 84
Rice Pudding, 201
Rice Wild with Mushrooms, 85

SALADS
Beet and Pear Salad, 50
Carrot-Pineapple Mold, 32
Catalina Carrots, 33
Dilled Cucumbers, 34
Fanciful Spinach Salad, 35
Greek Country Salad, 43
Hot Chevre over Greens, 45
Hot Potato Salad, 44
Hot Seafood Salad, 120

Jicama Medley, 31
Kiwi-Strawberry Salad, 42
Macaroni Salad, 46
Mozzarella and Tomato Salad, 48
Overnight Layered Salad, 47
Roasted Pepper Salad, 49
Ruby-Red Grapefruit and Onion, 36
Sauerkraut Mingle, 38
Shrimp and Tilsit Salad, 40
Snow Pea-Baby Corn Salad, 41
Spirited Italian Salad, 30
Tabbouli, 39
Tomatoes with Dill Cream, 37

SAUCES (also MARINADES)
Barbeque Ginger Sauce, 142
Barbeque Salmon Sauce, 117
Blueberry Duck Sauce, 146
Blueberry-Lemon Sauce, 153
Chicken, Anise Soya, 141
Chicken, Soya Honey, 144
Clam, Herbed for Pasta, 102
Cumberland Sauce, 27
Honey Garlic Glaze, 144
Lemon Lush for Fruit, 182
Mayonnaise, Green for Seafood, 126
Mayonnaise for Dip, 21
Mustard Dill Sauce, 22
Pesto, Basil for Pasta, 81
Pesto, Parsley for Pasta, 80
Raspberry Sauce for Berries, 180
Rum-Lime Sauce for Melons, 181
Teriyaki for Salmon, 118
Tomato-Lemon for Sausages, 23
Tomato Sauce for Mozzarella, 100
Tomato Sauce for Pizza, 165
Tzatziki for Souvlaki, 129
Whiskey Sauce for Pudding, 203

SEAFOOD (see FISH)

SIDE DISHES
Barley Mushroom Pilaf, 87
Bountiful Fried Rice, 83
Fettuccine and Green Cabbage, 89
Herbed Lemon Orzo, 86
Macaroni and Cheese, 88
Pesto for Pasta, 80-81
Refried Beans, 111
Rice Pilav with Currants, 84
Rice, Steamed the Easy Way, 82
Spaetzle with Spinach and Onions, 90
Wild Rice with Mushrooms, 85

SOUPS and STOCKS
Ace-in-the-Hole Clam Chowder, 76
Autumn Borscht, 77
Basic Chicken Stock, 78
Freshening Canned Broth, 78
Brandied Pumpkin Soup, 75
Cock-a-Leekie, 74
Cool Gazpacho, 73
Corn Kernel Soup, 71
Corn Oyster Soup, 71
Country-Style Split Pea, 70
Cream of Vegetable, 72
Garden Halibut Soup, 68
Some Turkey Soup!, 69

VEGETABLE ACCOMPANIMENTS
Asparagus with Pistachios, 63
Beets, Pickled, 64
Broccoli, Stir-Fried, 59
Cabbage, Red with Apples, 61
Carrot Marmalade, 66
Carrots, Orange Ginger, 56
Potato Jackets, Glorified, 52
Potato Latkes (Fritters), 54
Potatoes Boulangere, 55
Potatoes, Do-Ahead Whipped, 53
Rutabaga (Turnip) Puff, 57
Spinach with Bacon, Raisins, Nuts, 62
Tomatoes, Stuffed Provencale, 58
Vegetable Kebobs, Herbed, 65
Zucchini Boats, Stuffed, 60